Generous Justice

Also by Timothy Keller

The Reason for God: Belief in an Age of Scepticism
The Prodigal God: Recovering the Heart of the Christian Faith
Counterfeit Gods: When the Empty Promises of Love, Money, and
Power Let You Down

GENEROUS JUSTICE
How God's Grace Makes Us Just

Timothy Keller

HODDER &
STOUGHTON

First published by Dutton, a member of Penguin Group
(USA) Inc. in 2010

First published in Great Britain in 2010 by Hodder & Stoughton
An Hachette UK company

1

A CIP catalogue record for this title is available from the British Library

Hardback ISBN 978 0 340 99509 9
Trade Paperback ISBN 978 1 444 70210 1

Typeset in Gallard by Hewer Text UK Ltd, Edinburgh

Printed and bound by Clays Ltd, St Ives plc

Hodder & Stoughton policy is to use papers that are natural, renewable
and recyclable products and made from wood grown in sustainable
forests. The logging and manufacturing processes are expected to
conform to the environmental regulations of the country of origin.

Hodder & Stoughton Ltd
338 Euston Road
London NW1 3BH

www.hodderfaith.com

To the Deacons and Deaconesses
of Redeemer Presbyterian Church
and the leaders of Hope for New York,
with admiration and respect.

Contents

CONTENTS

INTRODUCTION

Why Write This Book?

Unrolling the scroll, he found the place where it is written: The Spirit of the Sovereign LORD is on me, because the LORD has anointed me to preach good news to the poor. He has sent me to bind up the broken-hearted, to proclaim freedom for the captives and release from darkness for the prisoners.

Luke 4:17–18

These are the words Jesus read in the synagogue in Nazareth when he announced the beginning of his ministry. He identified himself as the "Servant of the Lord," prophesied by Isaiah, who would "bring justice" to the world (Isaiah 42:1–7). Most people know that Jesus came to bring forgiveness and grace. Less well known is the Biblical teaching that a true experience of the grace of Jesus Christ inevitably motivates a man or woman to seek justice in the world.

While I was working on this volume, I heard two

questions from friends: "Who are you writing this for?" and "How did you come to be interested in the subject of justice?" The answers to these questions are a good way to introduce the book's themes.

Who Is This Book For?

There are four kinds of people who I hope will read this book. There is a host of young Christian believers who respond with joy to the call to care for the needy. Volunteerism is the distinguishing mark of an entire generation of American college students and recent graduates. The *NonProfit Times* reports that teens and young adults are leading "enormous spikes in applications to volunteer programs." Alan Solomont, chairman of the board of the Corporation for National and Community Service, says that "[this] younger generation . . . is more interested in service than other generations."[1] Volunteering rates among young adults dropped off significantly in the 1970s and 1980s, but "current youngsters grew up in schools that were more likely to have service learning programs . . . starting young people on a path of community service much earlier than before."[2]

As a pastor whose church is filled with young adults, I have seen this concern for social justice, but I also see many who do not let their social concern affect their personal lives. It does not influence how they spend money on themselves, how they conduct their careers, the way they choose and live in their neighborhoods, or whom they seek as friends. Also, many lose enthusiasm for volunteering over time.

From their youth culture they have imbibed not only an emotional resonance for social justice but also a consumerism that undermines self-denial and delayed gratification. Popular youth culture in Western countries cannot bring about the broad change of life in us that is required if we are to make a difference for the poor and marginalized. While many young adults have a Christian faith, and also a desire to help people in need, these two things are not actually connected to each other in their lives. They have not thought out the implications of Jesus's gospel for doing justice in all aspects of life. That connection I will attempt to make in this book.

Justice and the Bible

Another kind of person who I hope will read this book approaches the subject of "doing justice" with suspicion. In the twentieth century the American church divided between the liberal mainline that stressed social justice and the fundamentalist churches that emphasized personal salvation. One of the founders of the

Social Gospel movement was Walter Rauschenbusch, a German Baptist minister whose first pastorate was on the edge of New York City's Hell's Kitchen in the 1880s. His firsthand acquaintance with the terrible poverty of his neighborhood led him to question traditional evangelism, which took pains to save people's souls but did nothing about the social systems locking them into poverty. Rauschenbusch began to minister to "both soul and body," but in tandem with this shift in method came a shift in theology. He rejected the traditional doctrines of Scripture and atonement. He taught that Jesus did not need to satisfy the justice of God, and therefore he died only to be an example of unselfishness.[3]

In the mind of many orthodox Christians, therefore, "doing justice" is inextricably linked with the loss of sound doctrine and spiritual dynamism. However, Jonathan Edwards, the eighteenth-century author of the sermon "Sinners in the Hands of an Angry God," was a staunch Calvinist and hardly anyone's idea of a "liberal." Yet in his discourse on "The Duty of Charity to the Poor," he concluded, "Where have we any command in the Bible laid down in stronger terms, and in a more peremptory urgent manner, than the command of giving to the poor?"[4]

Unlike Rauschenbusch, Edwards argued that you did not have to change the classic Biblical doctrine of salvation to do ministry to the poor. On the contrary, such ministry flows directly out of historic evangelical teaching. He saw involvement with the poor and classic Biblical doctrine as indissolubly intertwined. That combination is relatively rare today, but it shouldn't be. I am writing this book for people who don't see yet what Edwards saw, namely, that when the Spirit enables us to understand what Christ has done for us, the result is a life poured out in deeds of justice and compassion for the poor.[5]

Others who I hope will give this book a hearing are the younger evangelicals who have "expanded their mission" to include social justice along with evangelism.[6] Many of them have not only turned away from older forms of ministry, but also from traditional evangelical doctrines of Jesus's substitutionary atonement and of justification by faith alone, which are seen as too "individualistic."[7] These authors usually argue that changes in theological emphasis—or perhaps outright changes in theological doctrine—are necessary if the church is going to be more engaged in the pursuit of social justice. The scope of the present volume prevents us from looking at these debates about atonement and justification. However, one of its main purposes is to show that such reengineering of doctrine is not only mistaken in itself, but also unnecessary. The most traditional formulation of evangelical doctrine, rightly understood, should lead its proponents to a life of doing justice in the world.

There is a fourth group of people who should find this book of interest. Recently there has been a rise in books and blogs charging that religion, to quote Christopher Hitchens, "poisons everything."[8] In their view religion, and especially the Christian church, is a primary force promoting injustice and violence on our planet. To such people the idea that belief in the Biblical God necessarily entails commitment to justice is absurd. But, as we will see, the Bible is a book devoted to justice in the world from first to last. And the Bible gives us not just a naked call to care about justice, but gives us everything we need—motivation, guidance, inner joy, and power—to live a just life.

I have identified four groups of readers who seem at first glance to be very different, but they are not. They all fail at some level to see that the Biblical gospel of Jesus necessarily and powerfully leads to a passion for justice in the world. A concern for justice in all aspects of life is neither an artificial add-on nor a contradiction to the message of the Bible.

Why Am I Interested in Justice?

How did I get interested in this subject? Practicing justice did not come naturally to me as a child. Growing up, I shunned the only child I knew well who was poor—Jeffrey, a boy in my elementary and middle-school classes who lived "under the Eighth Street Bridge." In my school's tightly ordered social system, there were the Insiders and Uncool Outsiders. Then there was Jeffrey, in a category by himself. His clothes were ill-fitting thrift store garments, and he smelled bad. He was mocked mercilessly, excluded from games and conversations, and penalized in classwork, since few wanted to cooperate with him on assignments and projects. I confess that I avoided him most of the time because I was one of the Uncool Outsiders and was hoping to improve my social status. Instead of identifying with Jeffrey and recognizing the injustice of how he was being treated, I turned on the only kid who was more of a social outsider than I was.[9]

When I entered college in the late 1960s, however, I became part of a generation of students transfixed by the Civil Rights Movement. I learned about the systematic violence that was being carried out against blacks and civil rights workers in the South. I remember being especially astonished by the image of James Meredith being gunned down in broad daylight on a voting rights march in 1966, with his assailant calmly looking on in one of the photographs. I was amazed that something as unjust as segregation could have been so easily rationalized by an entire society. It marked the first time I realized that most older white adults in my life were telling me things that were dead wrong. The problem was not just a "few troublemakers." Black people *did* have a right to demand the redress and rectifying of many wrongs.

"You're a Racist, You Know"

Although I had grown up going to church, Christianity began to lose its appeal to me when I was in college. One reason for my difficulty was the disconnect between my secular friends who supported the Civil Rights Movement, and the orthodox Christian believers who thought that Martin Luther King, Jr. was a threat to society. Why, I wondered, did the nonreligious believe so passionately in equal rights and justice, while the religious people I knew could not have cared less?

A breakthrough came when I discovered a small but thoughtful group of devout Christian believers who were integrating their faith with every kind of justice in society. At first I merely imported my views on racial justice and added them onto the theology I was learning as a Christian. I didn't see what later I came to realize, that in fact the Bible provides the very basis for justice. I learned that the creation account in Genesis was the origin for the idea of human rights in the West[10] and that Biblical prophetic literature rang with calls for justice. Years afterward I discovered that the Civil Rights Movement of the 1950s and '60s I so admired was grounded much more in the African-American church's Christian views of sin and salvation than in secularism.[11]

When I went to seminary to prepare for the ministry, I met an African-American student, Elward Ellis, who befriended both my future wife, Kathy Kristy, and me. He gave us gracious but bare-knuckled mentoring about the realities of injustice in American culture. "You're a racist, you know," he once said at our kitchen table. "Oh, you don't mean to be, and you don't want to be, but you are. You can't really help it." He said, for example, "When black people do things in a certain way, you say, 'Well, that's your culture.' But when white people do things in a certain way, you say, 'That's just the *right* way to do things.' You don't realize you really have a culture. You are blind to how many of your beliefs and practices are cultural." We began to see how, in so many ways, we made our cultural biases into moral principles and then judged people of other races as being inferior. His case was so strong and fair that, to our surprise, we agreed with him.

While I was in my first pastorate in Hopewell, Virginia, I decided to enroll in a doctor of ministry program, and my project (the "thesis" of the course) was on training deacons. In Presbyterian church organization there are two sets of officers—elders and deacons. Deacons had historically been designated to work with the poor and needy in the community, but over the years this legacy had been lost, and instead they had evolved into janitors and treasurers. My program advisor challenged me to study the history of the office and to develop ways to help Presbyterian churches recover this lost aspect of their congregational life.

I took the assignment, and it was a transformative process for me. I went to the social work department of a nearby university, got the full reading list for their foundational courses, and devoured all the books. I did historical research on how church deacons served as the first public social service structure in European cities such as Geneva, Amsterdam, and Glasgow. I devised courses of skill-training for deacons and wrote material to help church leaders get a vision not only for the "word" ministry of preaching and teaching, but also for "deed" ministry, serving people with material and economic needs.[12]

After my pastorate in Virginia, I went to teach at Westminster Seminary in Philadelphia. In my department were four faculty members who lived in the inner city and taught urban ministry. Each week I would go to the department meeting a bit early and have fifteen minutes or so alone talking with the chairman, Harvie Conn. Harvie was passionately committed to living and working in the city, and he was keenly aware of the systemic injustice in our society. As I look back on those times, I realize I was learning far more from him than at the time I thought I was. I read his little book *Evangelism: Doing Justice and Preaching Grace*[13] twenty-five years ago and its themes sank deep into my thinking about God and the church.

Inspired by Harvie's teaching and by all the experiences I had in urban churches in Philadelphia during the 1980s, I answered an invitation to move to the middle of New York City in 1989 and begin a new congregation, Redeemer Presbyterian Church.

On Grace and Being Just

There are many great differences between the small southern town of Hopewell, Virginia, and the giant metropolis of New York. But there was one thing that was exactly the same. To my surprise, there is a direct relationship between a person's grasp and experience of God's grace, and his or her heart for justice and the poor. In both settings, as I preached the classic message that God does *not* give us justice but saves us by free grace, I discovered that those most affected by the message became the most sensitive to the social inequities around them. One man in my church in Hopewell, Easley Shelton, went through a profound transformation. He moved out of a sterile, moralistic understanding of life and began to understand that his salvation was based on the free, unmerited grace of Jesus. It gave him a new warmth, joy, and confidence that everyone could see. But it had another surprising effect. "You know," he said to me one day, "I've been a racist all my life." I was startled, because I had not yet preached to him or to the congregation on that subject. He had put it together for himself. When he lost his Phariseeism, his spiritual self-righteousness, he said, he lost his racism.

Elaine Scarry of Harvard has written a fascinating little book called *On Beauty and Being Just*.[14] Her thesis is that the experience of beauty makes us less self-centered and more open to justice. I have observed over the decades that when people see the beauty of God's grace in Christ, it leads them powerfully toward justice.

This book, then, is both for believers who find the Bible a trustworthy guide and for those who wonder if Christianity is a positive influence in the world. I want the orthodox to see how central to the Scripture's message is justice for the poor and marginalized. I also want to challenge those who do not believe in Christianity to see the Bible not as a repressive text, but as the basis for the modern understanding of human rights. Throughout this book, I will begin each chapter with a call to justice taken directly from the Bible and show how these words can become the foundation of a just, generous human community. I don't expect to bring every reader all the way to agreement, but I do hope to introduce many to a new way of thinking about the Bible, justice, and grace.

GENEROUS JUSTICE

ONE

WHAT IS DOING JUSTICE?

*And what does the Lord require of you, but to do justice,
to love mercy, and to walk humbly with your God?*

Micah 6:8[15]

"I Didn't Know Who Was Going to Shoot Me First"

I recently met with Heather, a woman who attends my church in New York City. After graduating from Harvard Law School she landed a lucrative job with a major law firm in Manhattan. It was a dream come true for most aspiring young professionals. She was a high-powered corporate lawyer, she was "living the life" in the big city, and yet it was all strangely unsatisfying. She wanted to make a difference in the lives of individuals, and she was concerned about those in society who could not afford the kind of fees her clients paid her firm. For

[1]

a fraction of her former salary, she became an assistant district attorney for New York County, where so many of the criminals she prosecutes are those who have been exploiting the poor, particularly poor women.

When I was professor at a theological seminary in the mid-eighties, one of my students was a young man named Mark Gornik. One day we were standing at the copier and he told me that he was about to move into Sandtown, one of the poorest and most dangerous neighborhoods in Baltimore. I remember being quite surprised. When I asked him why, he said simply, "to do justice." It had been decades since any white people had moved *in*to Sandtown. For the first couple of years there it was touch and go. Mark told a reporter, "The police thought I was a drug dealer, and the drug dealers thought I was a police officer. So, for a while there, I didn't know who was going to shoot me first." Yet over the years Mark, along with leaders in the community, established a church and a comprehensive set of ministries that have slowly transformed the neighborhood.[16]

Although both Heather and Mark were living comfortable, safe lives, they became concerned about the most vulnerable, poor, and marginalized members of our society, and they made long-term personal sacrifices in order to serve their interests, needs, and cause.

That is, according to the Bible, what it means to "do justice."

What Is Doing Justice?

Justice Is Care for the Vulnerable

Micah 6:8 is a summary of how God wants us to live. To walk humbly with God is to know him intimately and to be attentive to what he desires and loves. And what does that consist of? The text says to "do justice and love mercy," which seem at first glance to be two different things, but they are not.[17] The term for "mercy" is the Hebrew word *chesedh*, God's unconditional grace and compassion. The word for "justice" is the Hebrew term *mishpat*. In Micah 6:8, "*mishpat* puts the emphasis on the action, *chesedh* puts it on the attitude [or motive] behind the action."[18] To walk with God, then, we must do justice, out of merciful love.

The word *mishpat* in its various forms occurs more than two hundred times in the Hebrew Old Testament. Its most basic meaning is to treat people equitably. So Leviticus 24:22 warns Israel to "have the same *mishpat* ["rule of law"] for the foreigner as the native." *Mishpat* means acquitting or punishing every person on the merits of the case, regardless of race or social status. Anyone who does the same wrong should be given the same penalty. But *mishpat* means more than just the punishment of wrongdoing. It also means to give people their rights. Deuteronomy 18 directs that the priests of the tabernacle should be supported by a certain percentage of the people's income. This support is described as "the priests' *mishpat*," which means their due or their right. So we read, "Defend the rights of the poor and needy" (Proverbs 31:9). *Mishpat*, then, is giving people what they are due, whether punishment or protection or care.

This is why, if you look at every place the word is used in the Old Testament, several classes of persons continually come up. Over and over again, *mishpat* describes taking up the care and cause of widows, orphans, immigrants, and the poor—those who have been called "the quartet of the vulnerable."[19]

> *This is what the LORD Almighty says:*
> *Administer true justice, show mercy and compassion to one another. Do not oppress the widow or the fatherless, the immigrant or the poor.*
>
> Zechariah 7:10–11

In premodern, agrarian societies, these four groups had no social power. They lived at subsistence level and were only days from starvation if there was any famine, invasion, or even minor social unrest. Today this quartet would be expanded to include the refugee, the migrant worker, the homeless, and many single parents and elderly people.

The *mishpat*, or justness, of a society, according to

the Bible, is evaluated by how it treats these groups. Any neglect shown to the needs of the members of this quartet is not called merely a lack of mercy or charity, but a violation of justice, of *mishpat*. God loves and defends those with the least economic and social power, and so should we. That is what it means to "do justice."

Justice Reflects the Character of God

Why should we be concerned about the vulnerable ones? It is because God is concerned about them. Consider the following texts:

*He executes justice [*mishpat*] for the oppressed and gives food to the hungry. The LORD sets prisoners free, the LORD gives sight to the blind, he lifts up those who are bowed down, the LORD loves those who live justly. The LORD watches over the immigrant and sustains the fatherless and the widow, but he frustrates the ways of the wicked.*

Psalm 146:7–9

*The LORD your God . . . defends the cause [*mishpat*] of the fatherless and the widow, and loves the immigrant, giving him food and clothing.*

Deuteronomy 10:17–18

[5]

It is striking to see how often God is introduced as the defender of these vulnerable groups. Don't miss the significance of this. When people ask me, "How do you want to be introduced?" I usually propose they say, "This is Tim Keller, minister at Redeemer Presbyterian Church in New York City." Of course I am many other things, but that is the main thing I spend my time doing in public life. Realize, then, how significant it is that the Biblical writers introduce God as "a father to the fatherless, a defender of widows" (Psalm 68:4–5). This is one of the main things he does in the world. He identifies with the powerless, he takes up their cause.

It is hard for us to understand how revolutionary this was in the ancient world. Sri Lankan scholar Vinoth Ramachandra calls this "scandalous justice." He writes that in virtually all the ancient cultures of the world, the power of the gods was channeled through and identified with the elites of society, the kings, priests, and military captains, not the outcasts. To oppose the leaders of society, then, was to oppose the gods. "But here, in Israel's rival vision," it is not high-ranking males but "the orphan, the widow, and the stranger" with whom Yahweh takes his stand. His power is exercised in history for their empowerment."[20] So, from ancient times, the God of the Bible stood out from the gods of all other religions as a God on the side of the powerless, and of justice for the poor.

What Is Doing Justice?

Is God on the Side of the Poor?

This emphasis in the Bible has led some, like Latin American theologian Gustavo Gutiérrez, to speak of God's "preferential option for the poor."[21] At first glance this seems to be wrong, especially in light of passages in the Mosaic law that warn against giving any preference to rich *or* poor (Leviticus 19:15; Deuteronomy 1:16–17). Yet the Bible says that God is the defender of the poor; it never says he is the defender of the rich. And while some texts call for justice for members of the well-off classes as well, the calls to render justice to the poor outnumber such passages by a hundred to one.

Why? Rich people can certainly be treated unjustly, but philosopher Nicholas Wolterstorff says it is a simple fact that the lower classes are "not only disproportionately vulnerable to injustice, but usually disproportionately actual victims of injustice. Injustice is not equally distributed."[22] It stands to reason that injustice is easier to perform against people without the money or social status to defend themselves. The poor cannot afford the best legal counsel, as my friend Heather knew very well. The poor are more often the victims of robbery, one of the most common forms of injustice, and ordinarily law enforcement is much quicker and more thorough in its response to violence against the rich and powerful than against the poor. Wolterstorff concludes, "One has to decide where lie the greatest injustices and where lies the greatest vulnerability. Other things being equal, one focuses one's attention on those."[23] In short, since most of the people who are downtrodden by abusive power are those who had little power to begin with, God gives them particular attention and has a special place in his heart for them. He says:

> *Speak up for those who cannot speak up for themselves, for the rights of all who are destitute. . . .*
>
> Proverbs 31:8

If God's character includes a zeal for justice that leads him to have the tenderest love and closest involvement with the socially weak, then what should God's people be like? They must be people who are likewise passionately concerned for the weak and vulnerable. God injected his concern for justice into the very heart of Israel's worship and community life with these texts:

> *Cursed be anyone who withholds the justice due to the immigrant, the fatherless, and the widow. Then all the people shall say, "Amen!"*
>
> Deuteronomy 27:19

[8]

What Is Doing Justice?

This is what the LORD says: "Do what is just and right. Rescue from the hand of his oppressor the one who has been robbed. Do no wrong or violence to the immigrant, the fatherless, or the widow, and do not shed innocent blood in this place."

Jeremiah 22:3

Israel was charged to create a culture of social justice for the poor and vulnerable because it was the way the nation could reveal God's glory and character to the world. Deuteronomy 4:6–8 is a key text where Israel is told that they should keep God's commands so that all the nations of the world will look at the justice and peace of their society, based on God's laws, and be attracted to God's wisdom and glory.[24]

This is why God can say that if we dishonor the poor we insult him, and when we are generous to the poor we honor him (Proverbs 14:31). If believers in God don't honor the cries and claims of the poor, we don't honor him, whatever we profess, because we hide his beauty from the eyes of the world. When we pour ourselves out for the poor—that gets the world's notice. Even when Christians were a small minority in the Roman Empire, their startling charity to the poor evoked great respect from the populace. To honor him we must defend the poor and needy (Jeremiah 22:16).

Justice Is Right Relationships

We must have a strong concern for the poor, but there is more to the Biblical idea of justice than that. We get more insight when we consider a second Hebrew word that can be translated as "being just," though it usually translated as "being righteous." The word is *tzadeqah*, and it refers to a life of right relationships. Bible scholar Alec Motyer defines "righteous" as those "right with God and therefore committed to putting right all other relationships in life." [25]

This means, then, that Biblical righteousness is inevitably "social," because it is about relationships. When most modern people see the word "righteousness" in the Bible, they tend to think of it in terms of private morality, such as sexual chastity or diligence in prayer and Bible study. But in the Bible *tzadeqah* refers to day-to-day living in which a person conducts *all* relationships in family and society with fairness, generosity, and equity. It is not surprising, then, to discover that *tzadeqah* and *mishpat* are brought together scores of times in the Bible.

These two words roughly correspond to what some have called "primary" and "rectifying justice." [26] Rectifying justice is *mishpat*. It means punishing wrongdoers and caring for the victims of unjust treatment. Primary justice, or *tzadeqah*, is behavior that, if it was

[10]

prevalent in the world, would render rectifying justice unnecessary, because everyone would be living in right relationship to everyone else.[27] Therefore, though *tzadeqah* is primarily about being in a right relationship with God, the righteous life that results is profoundly social. A passage in the book of Job illustrates what this kind of righteous or just-living person looks like:

> *I rescued the poor who cried for help, and the fatherless who had none to assist him. The man who was dying blessed me; I made the widow's heart sing. I put on righteousness* [tzadeqah] *as my clothing; justice* [mishpat] *was my robe and my turban. I was eyes to the blind and feet to the lame. I was a father to the needy; I took up the case of the immigrant. I broke the fangs of the wicked and snatched the victims from their teeth.*

Job 29:12–17

> *If I have denied justice* [mishpat] *to my menservants and maidservants when they had a grievance against me, what will I do when God confronts me? . . . If I have denied the desires of the poor or let the eyes of the widow grow weary, if I have kept my bread to myself, not sharing it with the fatherless— but from my youth I reared him as would a father, and from my birth I guided the widow—if I have*

seen anyone perishing for lack of clothing, or a needy man without a garment, and his heart did not bless me for warming him with the fleece from my sheep, if I have raised my hand against the fatherless, knowing that I had influence in court, then let my arm fall from the shoulder, let it be broken off at the joint. . . . these also would be sins to be judged, for I would have been unfaithful to God on high.

Job 31:13–28

Francis I. Anderson points out in his commentary on Job that this is one of the most important texts in the Scripture for the study of Israelite ethics. It is a complete picture of how a righteous Israelite was supposed to live, "and to [Job], right conduct is almost entirely social. . . . In Job's conscience . . . to omit to do good to any fellow human being, of whatever rank or class, would be a grievous offence to God."[28]

In Job's inventory of his life we see all the elements of what it means to live justly and do justice. We see direct, rectifying justice when Job says, "I took up the case of the immigrant; I broke the fangs of the wicked and snatched the victims from their teeth." This means Job confronted people who exploited the vulnerable. In our world, this could mean prosecuting the men who batter, exploit, and rob poor women. But it could also mean Christians respectfully putting pressure on a local police department until they respond to calls and crimes as quickly in the poor part of town as in the prosperous part. Another example would be to form an organization that both prosecutes and seeks against loan companies that prey on the poor and the elderly with dishonest and exploitive practices.

Job also gives us many examples of what we could call primary justice or righteous living. He says that he is "eyes to the blind and feet to the lame," and "a father to the needy." To be a "father" meant that he cared for the needs of the poor as a parent would meet the needs of his children.[29] In our world, this means taking the time personally to meet the needs of the handicapped, the elderly, or the hungry in our neighborhoods. Or it could mean the establishment of new nonprofits to serve the interests of these classes of persons. But it could also mean a group of families from the more prosperous side of town adopting the public school in a poor community and making generous donations of money and pro bono work in order to improve the quality of the education.

In chapter 31 Job gives us more details about a righteous or just life. He fulfills "the desires of the poor" (verse 16). The word "desire" does not mean just meeting basic needs for food and shelter. It means that he turns the poor man's life into a delight. Then he says that if he had not shared his bread or "the fleece from my sheep" with the poor, it would have been a terrible sin and offense to God (verses 23 and 28). This certainly goes beyond what today we would call "charity." Job is not just giving handouts, but rather has become deeply involved in the life of the poor, the orphaned, and the handicapped. His goal for the poor is a life of delight, and his goal for the widow is that her eyes would "no longer be weary." He is not at all satisfied with halfway measures for the needy people in his community. He is not content to give them small, perfunctory gifts in the assumption that their misery and weakness are a permanent condition.

When these two words, *tzadeqah* and *mishpat*, are tied together, as they are over three dozen times, the English expression that best conveys the meaning is "social justice."[30] It is an illuminating exercise to find texts where the words are paired and to then to translate the text using the term "social justice." Here are just two:

The Lord loves social justice; the earth is full of his unfailing love.

Psalms 33:5

And

This is what the LORD says: "Let not the wise man boast of his wisdom or the strong man boast of his

[14]

strength or the rich man boast of his riches, but let him who boasts boast about this: that he understands and knows me, that I am the LORD, who exercises kindness and social justice on earth, for in these I delight," declares the LORD.

Jeremiah 9:23–24

Justice Includes Generosity

Many readers may be asking at this point why we are calling private giving to the poor "justice." Some Christians believe that justice is strictly *mishpat*—the punishment of wrongdoing, period. This does not mean that they think that believers should be indifferent to the plight of the poor, but they would insist that helping the needy through generous giving should be called mercy, compassion, or charity, not justice. In English, however, the word "charity" conveys a good but optional activity. Charity cannot be a requirement, for then it would not be charity. But this view does not fit in with the strength or balance of the Biblical teaching.

In the Scripture, gifts to the poor are called "acts of righteousness," as in Matthew 6:1–2. Not giving generously, then, is not stinginess, but unrighteousness, a violation of God's law. Also, we looked at Job's description of all the things he was doing in order to live a just and righteous life in Job 31. He calls every failure to help the poor a sin, offensive to God's splendor (verse 23) and deserving of judgment and punishment (verse 28). Remarkably, Job is asserting that it would be a sin against God to think of his goods as belonging to himself alone. To not "share his bread" and his assets with the poor would be unrighteous, a sin against God, and therefore by definition a violation of God's justice.

Another passage, from the prophecy of Ezekiel, makes a very similar list to the one that we have in Job 31.

Suppose there is a righteous man [tzaddiq] who does what is just [mishpat] and right [tzadeqah]. He does not . . . oppress anyone, but returns what he took in pledge for a loan. He does not commit robbery but gives his food to the hungry and provides clothing for the naked. He does not lend at usury or take excessive interest.

Ezekiel 18:5, 7–8a

This just man does not use his economic position to exploit people who are in a weaker financial position. Most interesting is how the text pairs "he does not commit robbery" with the explanatory clause that he actively gives food and clothing to the poor. The implication is that if you do not actively and generously share your resources with the poor, you are a robber. You are not living justly.[31] This connection of generosity and care with *mishpat* is not confined to this text. Each of the following texts calls those who do justice to share their resources with the needy, because God does:

*He defends the cause [*mishpat*] of the fatherless and the widow, and loves the alien, giving him food and clothing. And you are to love those who are aliens, for you yourselves were aliens in Egypt.*

Deuteronomy 10:18–19

Is not this the kind of fasting I have chosen: to loose the chains of injustice and untie the cords of the yoke, to set the oppressed free and break every yoke? Is it not to share your food with the hungry and to provide the poor wanderer with shelter—when you see the naked, to clothe him. . . ?

Isaiah 58:6–7

Despite the effort to draw a line between "justice" as legal fairness and sharing as "charity," Ezekiel and Job make radical generosity one of the marks of living justly. The just person lives a life of honesty, equity, and generosity in every aspect of his or her life.

As we continue our study, we will see there are valid reasons why many become concerned when they hear Christians talk about "doing justice." Often that term is just a slogan being used to recruit listeners to jump on some political bandwagon. Nevertheless, if you are trying to live a life in accordance with the Bible, the concept and call to justice are inescapable. We do justice when we give all human beings their due as creations of God. Doing justice includes not only the righting of wrongs, but generosity and social concern, especially toward the poor and vulnerable. This kind of life reflects the character of God. It consists of a broad range of activities, from simple fair and honest dealings with people in daily life, to regular, radically generous giving of your time and resources, to activism that seeks to end particular forms of injustice, violence, and oppression.

TWO

※※

JUSTICE AND
THE OLD TESTAMENT

*All Scripture is given by inspiration of God,
and is profitable.*

2 Timothy 3:16

Christians and the Ceremonies

B efore looking at some other passages that show
how the Biblical concept of justice took form
in the society of Israel, we must consider the thorny
question: Are the laws of the Old Testament binding
on Christians today?

Even though Christians believe that all of Scripture
is authoritative, the coming of Christ fulfilled many of
the Old Testament laws in such a way that they no longer bear on believers directly. One clear example of
this is how the New Testament tells believers to regard
the "ceremonial" laws of Moses. The numerous "clean

laws" of Israel touching diet, dress, and other forms of ceremonial purity, as well as the entire sacrificial system and temple worship ordinances, are no longer considered binding on Christians, because Christ came and fulfilled them. In the New Testament book of Hebrews, we are told that Jesus is the final Sacrifice and the ultimate Priest, and so believers must no longer offer up animal sacrifices. Nor, as Jesus taught (Mark 7:17–23), do Christians have to obey the clean laws that determined if a worshipper was ceremonially clean and qualified for worship. Why not? It was because Christ's atoning sacrifice brings us the reality to which the sacrifices pointed, and in Christ believers are permanently made "clean" and acceptable in God's sight.

Nevertheless, as Biblical scholar Craig Blomberg points out, "Every command [from the Old Testament] reflects principles at some level that are binding on Christians (2 Timothy 3:16)."[32] That is, even the parts of the Old Testament that are now fulfilled in Christ still have some abiding validity. For example, the principle of offering God sacrifices still remains in force, though changed by Christ's work. We are now required to offer God our entire lives as sacrifices (Romans 12:1–2), as well as the sacrifices of worship to God and the sharing of our resources with others (Hebrews 13:5).

And consider the book of Leviticus with all its clean laws and ceremonial regulations. These laws are not directly binding on Christians, but when Paul makes his case that Christians should lead holy lives, sharply distinct from those of the nonbelieving culture around them, he quotes Leviticus 26:12. (See 2 Corinthians 6:16–17.) So the coming of Christ changes the *way* in which Christians exhibit their holiness and offer their sacrifices, yet the basic principles remain valid.

Christians and the Civil Law of Moses

However, our concern here is not the ceremonial laws of Moses. What about the "civil" laws, the laws of social justice that have to do with the forgiving of debts, the freeing of slaves, and the redistribution of wealth? In the Old Testament believers comprised a single nation-state, with divinely appointed land apportionments and with a religious law code backed up by civil sanctions. Israel was characterized by theocratic rule in which both idolatry and adultery were offenses punished by the state. But in the New Testament this changed. Christians now do not constitute a theocratic kingdom-state, but exist as an international communion of local assemblies living in every nation and culture, under many different governments to whom they give great respect but never absolute allegiance. Jesus's famous teaching to "render to Caesar the things that are Caesar's, and to God the things that are God's"

(Matthew 22:21) signaled this change in the relationship between church and state to one of "nonestablishment."

Though believers are still a "covenant community," a people who are bound together to obey God's will, the church is not the state. So the apostle Paul, for example, calls for the rebuke of an adulterer in the Corinthian church. And if he does not repent, says Paul, expel him from membership in the community (1 Corinthians 5). Nevertheless, Paul does not demand his execution, as would have been the case in Israel. The church is not a government that rewards virtue and punishes evildoers with coercive force. But despite this massive change, do we have reason to believe that the civil laws of Moses, though not binding, still have some abiding validity? Yes.

Several factors should guide us. We should be wary of simply saying, "These things don't apply anymore," because the Mosaic laws of social justice are grounded in God's character, and that never changes. God often tells the Israelites to lend to the poor without interest and to distribute goods to the needy and to defend the fatherless, because "the LORD your God . . . defends the cause [*mishpat*] of the fatherless and the widow, and loves the alien, giving him food and clothing" (Deuteronomy 10:17–18). If this is true of God, we who believe in him must always find some way of expressing it our own practices, even if believers now live in a new stage in the history of God's redemption.

Also, in the next chapters we will see that New Testament writers do continue to look back to these social justice laws and base practices within the New Testament church upon them. For example, though the laws of gathering manna in the wilderness are obviously not applicable today, in 2 Corinthians 8:13–15 Paul can use them to require economic sharing and radical generosity among Christians. Just as Israel was a "community of justice," so the church is to reflect these same concerns for the poor.

Christians and Society

But even if we can apply the social legislation of Old Testament Israel in some ways to the New Testament church, can we apply it to our society at large? Here we must be far more cautious. The laws of social justice in Israel were principles for relationships primarily between believers. Israel was a nation-state in which every citizen was bound to obey the whole law of God and also was required to give God wholehearted worship. This is not the situation in our society today.

Nevertheless, the Bible gives us an example of a believer calling a nonbelieving king to stop ruling unjustly (Daniel 4:27). In the book of Amos, we see God holding nonbelieving nations accountable for oppression, injustice, and violence (Amos 1:3–2:3). It is clearly God's will that all societies reflect his concern for justice for the weak and vulnerable. So, like the ceremonial laws, the civil laws have some abiding validity that believers must carefully seek to reflect in their own lives and practices, not only as members of the church, but as citizens of their countries.

For example, many Biblical passages warn judges and rulers against taking bribes. "Do not pervert justice [*mishpat*] or show partiality. Do not accept a bribe, for a bribe blinds the eyes of the wise and twists the words of the righteous" (Deuteronomy 16:19). The poor person cannot afford to offer incentives to lawmakers and judges to decide matters for his benefit, but the rich and powerful can do this, and this is why bribery is so heinous to God. It marginalizes the poor from power. Bribery, of course, can take many modern forms. Poor people cannot make major contributions to a legislator's campaign fund, for example. Do we want to say that these laws against bribery have no abiding validity? Should we insist that Christians should not try to see our own society's laws reflect this particular kind of Biblical righteousness? Of course not.

With these caveats and cautions in mind, then, let's look at the kind of society God called Israel to be, and see what we can learn from it.

A Community of Justice

One of the best places to see what God's just society was supposed to look like is Deuteronomy 15. Here we read two verses that seem at first glance to be in tension with each other. In verse 11 it says, "There will always be poor people in the land, therefore I command you to be openhanded . . . toward the poor and needy in your land." Yet just before, we read this:

There should be no poor among you, for in the land the LORD your God is giving you to possess as your inheritance, he will richly bless you, if only you fully obey the LORD your God and are careful to follow all these commands I am giving you today.

Deuteronomy 15:4–5

Despite the initial appearance, there is no contradiction. Surrounding verses 4 and 5 are a set of laws known as *"shemitta"* law, from the Hebrew word for "release." At the beginning of the chapter we read:

At the end of every seven years you must cancel debts. [Literally make a "release," shemitta.] This is how it is to be done: Every creditor shall cancel any loan he has made to his fellow Israelite.

Deuteronomy 15:1–2

This directed that any Israelite who fell into debt had to be forgiven those debts every seventh year. Not only could creditors no longer demand payment, but they had to release the pledges of collateral taken for the debt. Collateral was usually a portion of land from which produce could have been used to repay the loan.[33] This law of release was a powerful and specific public policy aimed at removing one of the key factors causing poverty—long-term, burdensome debt.

Later, in verses 7 through 11, using emphatic Hebrew constructions that can only be conveyed in English with lots of adverbs, such as "richly" (verse 4), "fully" (verse 5), "freely" (verse 8), and "generously" (verse 10), there was a powerful call to give to and help the poor until their need is eliminated.

If there is a poor man among your brothers in any of the towns of the land that the LORD your God is giving you, do not be hardhearted or tightfisted toward your poor brother. Rather be openhanded and freely lend him whatever he needs.

Deuteronomy 15:7–8

The poor man was not to be given merely a token "handout." Rather, credit and help were to be extended until he was completely out of poverty. The generosity extended to the poor could not be cut off until the poor person's need was gone and until he reached a level of self-sufficiency. Now we can understand how the passage could say, "There should be no poor among you." God's concern for the poor is so strong that he gave Israel a host of laws that, if practiced, would have virtually eliminated any permanent underclass.

Besides the laws of release, there were the laws of "gleaning." Landowners could not gather all the grain their land could produce. They had to leave some of it for the poor to gather themselves (Leviticus 19:9–10; 23:22). In other words, they were to voluntarily limit their profit-taking. Gleaning was not, however, what would ordinarily be called an act of charity. It enabled the poor to provide for themselves without relying on benevolence. On the other hand, Deuteronomy 23:24–25 protected the landowner from those who might try to overglean. The Bible is not a classist tract that sees the rich as always the villains and the poor as always virtuous.

In addition, there were the laws of tithing. All Israelites gave one-tenth of their annual income to the Levites and priests for the upkeep of the temple.[34] However, every third year the tithes were put in public storehouses so that the poor and "the aliens, the fatherless, and the widows" would receive them (Deuteronomy 14:29).[35]

Lastly, there was the remarkable "year of Jubilee."

[27]

Every seventh year was a "Sabbath" year in which debts and slaves were freed (Deuteronomy 15:1–18).[36] But every seventh Sabbath year (every forty-ninth year) was declared a "Jubilee." In that year not only were debts to be forgiven, but the land was to go back to its original tribal and family allotments made when the Israelites returned to the land out of Egypt. Over a fifty-year period some families would economically do better and acquire more land while others would fare more poorly and have to sell some of their land— or lose it altogether and become workers and servants. But every fifty years the land was to go back to its original owners (Leviticus 25:8–55).

"Here, if ever," writes Craig Blomberg, "is the ultimate relativization of private property. On average, each person or family had at least a once-in-a-lifetime chance to start afresh, no matter how irresponsibly they had handled their finances or how far into debt they had fallen."[37]

If we combine the requirements of radical generosity with the regulations on profit-taking and property use, we are not surprised that God could say, "There should be no poor among you." This does not mean that people would not continue to fall into poverty. But if Israel as an entire society had kept God's laws perfectly with all their hearts, there would have been no permanent, long-term poverty.

Justice and Our Political Categories

We now need to face one of the main concerns of those who object to Christians talking so much of "social justice." Kevin DeYoung states the problem in this way:

> While the general principle—help the poor, don't harm them—is abundantly and repeatedly clear in Scripture, the application of this principle is less so. For example, does a passage like Isaiah 58 support state-sponsored redistribution efforts? Christians can and do argue for this, but this text certainly doesn't require this solution to poverty.

Deuteronomy 15 and the other Mosaic legislation that we have surveyed seem to answer DeYoung's question with a "yes." Israel did redistribute money, assets, and even land from the well-off to the poor, with the help of state-sponsored laws and institutions.

But as we've pointed out, Israel was a theocratic nation-state in covenant with God. We do not have anything like this today. We have been arguing that everything in the Old Testament has some abiding validity, though it must be applied with great care. Take the laws of gleaning, for example. I know of no one who believes that the Bible requires Christians to turn

Old Testament gleaning into law in the United States. But what do the gleaning laws reveal to us about God's will for our relationships? Why was it that landowners were not allowed to harvest out to the margins of their field? God did not want them to squeeze every cent of profit out of their land, and then think that by giving to charity they were doing all they could for general community welfare. The gleaning laws enabled the poor to be self-sufficient, not through getting a handout, but through their own work in the field.

How can business owners follow the same principles today? They should not squeeze every penny of profit out of their businesses for themselves by charging the highest possible fees and prices to customers and paying the lowest possible wages to workers. Instead, they should be willing to pay higher wages and charge lower prices that in effect share the corporate profits with employees and customers, with the community around them. This always creates a more vibrant, strong human community. How could a government follow the gleaning principle? It would do so by always favoring programs that encourage work and self-sufficiency rather than dependency.

For another example, see how Paul uses Exodus 16:18 in 2 Corinthians 8. In the desert God provided for the material needs of the people with manna that appeared in the mornings and that had to be gathered. Even though some were more able gatherers of manna than others, all manna was distributed equitably so that no one received too much or too little for their needs (Exodus 16:16–18). Any manna that was hoarded simply spoiled—it became rancid and full of maggots (verses 19–21). In 2 Corinthians 8:13–15 Paul interprets this as an abiding principle for how we are to deal with God's material provision for us. He likens our money to manna. Paul teaches that the money we have is as much a gift of God as the manna was a gift to the Israelites in the desert. Though some are more able "gatherers"—that is, some are better at making money than others—the money you earn is a gift of God. Therefore, the money you make must be shared to build up community. So wealthier believers must share with poorer ones, not only within a congregation but also across congregations and borders. (See 2 Corinthians 8:15 and its context.) To extend the metaphor—money that is hoarded for oneself rots the soul.

We have seen a number of ways in which the social justice legislation of the Old Testament has abiding validity, yet we must recognize that everything I have just outlined is inferential. The Bible has many very direct and clear ethical prescriptions for human life. But when we come to the Old Testament social legislation, the application must be done with care and it will always be subject to debate. For example, while we have seen that the Bible demands that we share our resources with the needy, and that to fail to do so is unjust, taken as a whole the Bible does not say precisely how that redistribution should be carried out. Should it be the way political conservatives prescribe, almost exclusively through voluntary, private giving? Or should it be the way that political liberals desire, through progressive taxation and redistribution by the state? Thoughtful people have and will argue about which is the most effective way to help the poor. Both sides looking for support in the Bible can find some, and yet in the end what the Bible says about social justice cannot be tied to any one political system or economic policy. If it is possible, we need to take politics out of this equation as we look deeper into the Bible's call for justice.

In Craig Blomberg's survey of the Mosaic laws of gleaning, releasing, tithing, and the Jubilee, he concludes that the Biblical attitude toward wealth and possessions does not fit into any of the normal categories of democratic capitalism, or of traditional monarchial feudalism, or of state socialism. The rules for the use of land in the Biblical laws challenge all major contemporary economic models. They "suggest a sharp critique of 1) the statism that disregards the precious treasure of personal rootage, and 2) the untrammeled individualism which secures individuals at the expense of community."[38]

What Causes Poverty?

One of the main reasons we cannot fit the Bible's approach into a liberal or conservative economic model is the Scripture's highly nuanced understanding of the causes of poverty. Liberal theorists believe that the "root causes" of poverty are always social forces beyond the control of the poor, such as racial prejudice, economic deprivation, joblessness, and other inequities. Conservative theorists put the blame on the breakdown of the family, the loss of character qualities such as self-control and discipline, and other habits and practices of the poor themselves.

By contrast, the causes of poverty as put forth in the Bible are remarkably balanced. The Bible gives us a matrix of causes. One factor is oppression, which includes a judicial system weighted in favor of the powerful (Leviticus 19:15), or loans with excessive interest (Exodus 22:25–27), or unjustly low wages (Jeremiah 22:13; James 5:1–6). Ultimately, however, the prophets blame the rich when extremes of wealth and poverty in society appear (Amos 5:11–12; Ezekiel 22:29; Micah 2:2; Isaiah 5:8). As we have seen, a great deal of the Mosaic legislation was designed to keep the ordinary disparities between the wealthy and the poor from becoming aggravated and extreme. Therefore, whenever great disparities arose, the prophets assumed that to some degree it was the result of selfish individualism rather than concern with the common good.

If this were all that the Bible had to say about poverty, we might be tempted to assume that the liberals were right, that poverty comes from only unjust social conditions. But there are other factors. One is what we could call "natural disasters." This refers to any natural circumstance that brings or keeps a person in poverty, such as famine (Genesis 47), disabling injury, floods, or fires. It may be fair to say, also, that some people lack the ability to make wise decisions. It is not a moral failing, they are simply unable to make good choices because they lack insight.[39]

Another cause of poverty, according to the Bible, is what we could call "personal moral failures," such as indolence (Proverbs 6:6–7), and other problems with self-discipline (Proverbs 23:21). The book of Proverbs is particularly forceful in its insistence that hard work can lead to economic prosperity (Proverbs 12:11; 14:23; 20:13), though there are exceptions (Proverbs 13:23).

Poverty, therefore, is seen in the Bible as a very complex phenomenon. Several factors are usually intertwined.[40] Poverty cannot be eliminated simply by personal initiative or by merely changing the tax structure. Multiple factors are usually interactively present in the life of a poor family. For example: A person raised in a racial/economic ghetto (factor #1) is likely to have poor health (factor #2) and also learn many habits that do not fit with material/social advancement (factors #2 and 3). Any large-scale improvement in a society's level of poverty will come through a comprehensive array of public and private, spiritual, personal, and corporate measures. There are many indications that scholars are coming to have a more balanced, complex view of poverty and are breaking through the older Right-Left deadlock.[41]

A Case Study

Mark Gornik, who I introduced in chapter 1 and who is a founder of New Song Church and ministries in Baltimore, makes a compelling case that "systematic exclusion" creates many poor inner-city neighborhoods. He uses the history of his former neighborhood, Sandtown, as an example. In the early and mid-twentieth century, the neighborhoods east of Sandtown, near the industrial jobs in the city's center, were reserved for white immigrants, and the more prosperous neighborhoods to the west were also for whites only. Segregation saw to this. African-American newcomers from the South had to move into Sandtown, a place where the only jobs available were as low-wage domestic workers for wealthier families to the west. Many white-owned businesses would not hire African-Americans at all, or they did so for only menial work. Sandtown landlords shoehorned people into overcrowded and substandard housing. "This combination of circumstances led to a subsistence existence."[42]

By the 1970s, the industrial and manufacturing job base of the city of Baltimore was in sharp decline. New jobs were created in the suburbs and exurbs, places that were too expensive for many urban residents to live and inaccessible to them by transportation lines. The new jobs that were produced required advanced degrees, since the culture was shifting from a manu- facturing to a service and knowledge economy. In just fifteen years, jobs in the city that required only a high school education (blue collar jobs) decreased by 45 percent, while jobs that required training past high school or college increased 56 percent.[43] Residents of inner-city neighborhoods, with their weak and failing schools, were completely unequipped to make the shift toward these jobs with the rest of society. Lower pay- ing service-sector jobs were all that was left, without the retirement and health benefits and job security of the older manufacturing jobs, and those better-paying manufacturing jobs disappeared altogether for the res- idents of Sandtown.[44] Many people just gave up on finding formal work.

The resulting economic weakness in the neighbor- hood led to the kind of exploitative behavior toward the poor that the Bible condemns. Landlords did not live in the neighborhood. They provided abysmal services and maintenance, or abandoned their buildings altogether. Banks and lending institutions engaged in various forms of redlining, making it impossible for neighborhood residents to get home loans or insurance or credit cards.[45] Crime rose and the victims were usually members of the neighborhood. Businesses that were important for healthy communities moved out, and in their place came gun dealers, check-cashing centers, liquor stores, and porn shops, all of which encouraged the worst kinds of behavior in urban residents.[46]

During the middle and late twentieth century, government policy encouraged middle-class people to leave the city, further isolating communities like Sandtown. For example, intrusive freeways were built to enable people to live in the suburbs and commute by car to center city jobs, and many of these building programs bisected or devastated urban neighborhoods, as chronicled in Robert Caro's classic *The Power Broker: Robert Moses and the Fall of New York*.[47]

Gornik's research and narrative make a convincing case—the poverty of an inner-city neighborhood like Sandtown was not initially the product of individual irresponsible behavior or family breakdown. A complex range of structural factors led to the exclusion of the neighborhood's residents from the resources they needed to thrive. And before that, the poverty of African-Americans emigrating into Baltimore from the South was due in great part to the legacy of slavery and Jim Crow laws. But the results of these factors were addiction, family breakdown, criminal activity, depression, the disintegration of community, and the erosion of personal character. This is why the problems of the poor are so much more complex than any one theory can accommodate. What it takes to rebuild a poor neighborhood goes well beyond public policy or social programs. It takes the rebuilding of families and communities and individual lives. This is why Gornik not only established programs of social service, but he also began a church that called people to spiritual conversion.[48]

The three causes of poverty, according to the Bible, are oppression, calamity, and personal moral failure. Having surveyed the Bible on these texts numerous times, I have concluded that the emphasis is usually on the larger structural factors. In many countries of the world, corrupt governments, oppressive economic orders, and natural disasters keep hundreds of millions of people in poverty. In our own country, the weak educational system that society provides for inner city youth sets them up for failure. But when we add personal wrongdoing and crime to the larger forces of exclusion and oppression, we have a potent mixture that locks people into poverty. Taken in isolation no one factor—government programs, public policy, calls to personal responsibility, or private charity—is sufficient to address the problem.

"If He Cannot Afford . . ."

In an out-of-the-way part of the Hebrew Bible, in Leviticus 5, there are prescriptions for making confessions and offering sacrifices to God at the tabernacle in order to seek forgiveness for sins. There is an eye-glazing number of diverse rules and regulations for how to make atonement for various sins—what the penitents must do, what kind of animal sacrifices they had to bring, what the priests had to do, and so on. Then suddenly the text adds that if the worshipper "cannot afford" the standard offerings, "he is to bring as an offering a tenth of an *ephah* of fine flour for a sin offering. . . . In this way the priest will make atonement for him for any of these sins he has committed, and he will be forgiven" (Leviticus 5:11–13). One Bible commentary responds to this:

> A person who knew he could come to God with nothing more than a cupful of flour and a confession of his sin and still receive forgiveness was learning something fundamental about the grace

of God . . . even the most powerful in the land knew that God was not impressed by the most lavish sacrifices. . . .[49]

Remember what Vinoth Ramachandra said. In the religions of the surrounding cultures, the gods identified particularly with the kings and others at the top of society. It made sense—the rich could build the gods magnificent temples and give sumptuous offerings. Why wouldn't they be considered the favorites of the gods? But the Biblical God is not like that at all. He does not call everyone to bring sacrifices of the same kind and value, for that would have automatically make it easier for the rich to please God. Instead, God directs that each person should bring what they can, and if their heart is right, that will give them access to his grace.

For indeed, grace is the key to it all. It is not our lavish good deeds that procure salvation, but God's lavish love and mercy. That is why the poor are as acceptable before God as the rich. It is the generosity of God, the freeness of his salvation, that lays the foundation for the society of justice for all. Even in the seemingly boring rules and regulations of tabernacle rituals, we see that God cares about the poor, that his laws make provision for the disadvantaged. God's concern for justice permeated every part of Israel's life. It should also permeate our lives.

THREE

WHAT DID JESUS SAY
ABOUT JUSTICE?

*When you give a luncheon or dinner, do not invite
your friends, your brothers or relatives, or your rich
neighbors; if you do, they may invite you back and so
you will be repaid. But when you give a banquet, invite the poor, the crippled, the lame and the blind. . . .*

Luke 14:12–13

"But That's the Old Testament!"

When I was a young pastor at my first church in
Hopewell, Virginia, a single mother with four
children began attending our services. It became clear
very quickly that she had severe financial problems,
and several people in the church proposed that we
try to help her. By that time I had begun to share my
doctoral research with some of the church's deacons. I
pointed out that historically church deacons had given
aid in exactly these circumstances. So the deacons vis-

ited her and offered to give her church funds for several months to help her pay off outstanding bills. She happily accepted. Three months later it came out that, instead of paying her bills with the money we had been giving her, she had spent it on sweets and junk food, had gone out to restaurants with her family multiple times, and had bought each child a new bike. Not a single bill had been paid, and she needed more money.

One of the deacons was furious. "No way do we give her any more," he said to me. "This is the reason that she's poor—she's irresponsible, driven by her impulses! That was God's money and she wasted it." I countered with some passages from the Bible on doing justice for the fatherless and the needy. "But that's the *Old* Testament," he said, and argued that today it was Christians' job to spread the good news about Jesus. "Christians should not be concerned about poverty and social conditions, but about saving souls."

We have been making the case that the Bible calls us to be deeply involved in defending and caring for the poor, but indeed, we have so far looked at the Hebrew Scriptures, that part of the Bible that Christians call the Old Testament. My deacon was not a trained theologian, but his intuition is a common one, namely that while the Old Testament talks a lot about evil and justice, Jesus talks mainly about love and forgiveness. Anders Nygren, the influential author of *Agape and Eros,* published in the 1930s, argued this forcefully at a scholarly level. "God's attitude to men is not characterized by *justitia distributiva,* but by agape [love], not by retributive righteousness, but by freely giving and forgiving love."[50] Nygen's argument was that, for God, love and justice are mutually exclusive, they don't mix at all. In this view Christ has overcome justice and now all our relationships should be based on spontaneous love and generosity, not justice. Justice is all about "rights" and legal obligations, but Christ's salvation is a grace that is undeserved. Christians should not be concerned with getting people their rights. The gospel is about love and service, about forgiveness and caring for people regardless of their rights.

Jesus and the Vulnerable

This reasoning seems plausible at first glance. However, when we study the gospels we find that Jesus has not "moved on" at all from the Old Testament's concern for justice. In fact, Jesus has an intense interest in and love for the same kinds of vulnerable people. Nor can it be argued that this concern is a lower priority for Jesus. When some of John the Baptist's disciples came and asked him if he truly was the Messiah, he said:

Go back and report to John what you hear and see: The blind receive sight, the lame walk, those who

have leprosy are cured, the deaf hear, the dead are
raised, and the good news is preached to the poor.

Matthew 11:4–5

Here is the same care for the vulnerable that characterizes the heart of God. While clearly Jesus was preaching the good news to all, he showed throughout his ministry the particular interest in the poor and the downtrodden that God has always had.

Jesus, in his incarnation, "moved in" with the poor. He lived with, ate with, and associated with the socially ostracized (Matt 9:13). He raised the son of the poor widow (Luke 7:11–16) and showed the greatest respect to the immoral woman who was a social outcast (Luke 7:36ff). Indeed, Jesus spoke with women in public, something that a man with any standing in society would not have done, but Jesus resisted the sexism of his day (John 4:27).[51] Jesus also refused to go along with the racism of his culture, making a hated Samaritan the hero of one of his most famous parables (Luke 10:26ff) and touching off a riot when he claimed that God loved Gentiles like the widow of Zarephath and Naaman the Syrian as much as Jews (Luke 4:25–27). Jesus showed special concern for children, despite his apostles' belief that they were not worth Jesus's time (Luke 18:15).

Lepers also figured greatly in Jesus's ministry. They

were not only sick and dying, but were the outcasts of society. Jesus not only met their need for physical healing, but reached out his hand and touched them, giving them their first human contact in years (Mark 1:41; Luke 5:13). He called his disciples to give to the poor in the strongest and most startling ways, while praising the poor for their own generosity (Mark 12:42–43).

His own mother prophesied that he would "fill the poor" but turn the rich away empty (Luke 1:53). Yet Jesus also showed true justice by opening his arms to several classes of people who were not just poor. He ate with and spoke to tax collectors, the wealthiest people in society, yet the most hated, since they acquired their gains through collaborating with the Roman forces of occupation. The first witnesses to Jesus's birth were shepherds, a despised group considered unreliable, yet God revealed the birth of his son first to them. The first witnesses of Jesus's resurrection were women, another class of people so marginalized that their testimony was not admissible evidence in court. Yet Jesus revealed himself to them first. The examples are too many too enumerate.

Look at two of Jesus's directions to his followers regarding the poor. In Luke 14, he challenged people to routinely open their homes and purses to the poor, the blind, and the maimed.

When you give a luncheon or dinner, do not invite your friends, your brothers or relatives, or your rich neighbors; if you do, they may invite you back and so you will be repaid. But when you give a banquet, invite the poor, the crippled, the lame, and the blind. . . .

Luke 14:12–13

The great eighteenth-century hymn-writer and ex–slave trader John Newton marveled at the far-reaching implications of these words. "One would almost think that Luke 14:12–14 was not considered part of God's word," he wrote, "nor has any part of Jesus's teaching been more neglected by his own people. I do not think it is unlawful to entertain our friends; but if these words do not teach us that it is in some respects our duty to give a *preference* to the poor, I am at a loss to understand them."[52]

What was Jesus saying here? Later in this same chapter, Jesus tells his disciples that they must "hate" their fathers and mothers if they are going to follow him (Luke 14:26). This sounds shocking to us, but it is a Semitic idiomatic expression. Jesus did not mean literally that we should hate our parents, since this would contradict his own teaching (Mark 7:9–13) and the Ten Commandments. Rather, the expression meant that your love and loyalty for Jesus should so exceed all other loyalties that they look like "hate" by comparison. This way of speaking sheds light on Jesus's statement about banquets.

In Jesus's day, society operated largely on a patronage system. People with means created influence networks by opening doors and giving resources to people who in turn provided business opportunities and political favors, and watched out for their patron's interests. In this kind of culture, banquets were necessary. They were expensive, but they paid off because that was the way that business was done. Dinners were ways to sustain and reward current patronage relationships and also were opportunities for creating new ones. That is why the only people you invited were your own peers and existing relations, as well as "your rich neighbors."

Jesus's advice would have looked like economic and social suicide. He commanded that his disciples should share their homes and build relationships not with people from their own social class (or higher) who would profit them, but with people who were poor and without influence, who could never pay them back with money or favors. When Jesus said, "don't invite your friends for dinner" he should not be taken literally, any more than when he said we should hate our father and our mother. Indeed, Jesus often ate meals in homes with his friends and peers. Rather—to put this in a more modern context—he is saying that we should spend *far* more of our money and wealth on the poor than we do on our own entertainment, or on vacations, or on eating out and socializing with important peers.

Jesus bluntly and shockingly contradicted the spirit and practice of the patronage system of his day, telling his disciples to give without expecting repayment (Luke 6:32–36; 14:13–14) and, if possible, in secret (Matthew 6:1–4). His followers' help of the poor was thus motivated by a sense of simple justice (e.g., Luke 18:1–8) and a real concern to alleviate misery (e.g., Luke 10:25–37, *"mercy"*). The patronage system was characterized by neither compassion nor justice. It did not unite a society divided by class and race—it sustained the status quo. Jesus's ethic of love attacked the world system at its root.

In a second passage, Jesus exhorts his disciples to "sell your possessions and give to the poor. Provide purses for yourselves that will not wear out, a treasure in heaven that will not be exhausted, where no thief comes near and no moth destroys" (Luke 12:33). He also famously told the rich young ruler to sell *all* his possessions and give them to the poor (Matthew 19:21; Luke 18:22). What do we say to such strong injunctions? It can be argued that the command to the rich young ruler was not universal. As evidence, we can point to Jesus's encounter with the rich tax collector Zacchaeus, who, when converted, happily told

Jesus that he was giving one half of all his wealth to the poor. Jesus responded positively. He didn't say, "No, that's not enough." What is Jesus's point, then, in these exhortations? It must be *at least* this—that his believers should not see any of their money as their own, and they should be profoundly involved with and generous to the poor.

Jesus and the Prophets

Jesus not only shared the Old Testament's zeal for the cause of the vulnerable, he also adopted the prophets' penetrating use of justice as heart-analysis, the sign of true faith. At first glance, no two things can seem more opposed than grace and justice. Grace is giving benefits that are not deserved, while justice is giving people exactly what they do deserve. In Christ we receive grace, unmerited favor. Nevertheless, in the mind of the Old Testament prophets as well as the teaching of Jesus, an encounter with grace inevitably leads to a life of justice.

Isaiah, Jeremiah, Zechariah, and Micah all leveled the charge that, while the people attended worship, observed all religious regulations, and took pride in their Biblical knowledge, nevertheless they took advantage of the weak and vulnerable. The prophets concluded that, therefore, their religious activity was not

just insufficient, it was deeply offensive to God. In Isaiah chapters 1 and 58 the message is chilling:

> *When you spread out your hands in prayer, I will*
> *hide my eyes from you. . . . Your hands are full of*
> *blood. . . . Learn to do right! Seek justice* [mish-
> pat]*, encourage the oppressed. Defend the father-*
> *less, plead the case of the widow.*
>
> Isaiah 1:17

> *Is not this the kind of fasting I have chosen: to loose*
> *the chains of injustice and untie the cords of the*
> *yoke, to set the oppressed free and break every yoke?*
> *Is it not to share your food with the hungry and to*
> *provide the poor wanderer with shelter . . . ?*
>
> Isaiah 58:6–7

The implications of this accusation are clear. Justice
is not just one more thing that needs to be added to the
people's portfolio of religious behavior. A lack of justice is a sign that the worshippers' hearts are not right
with God at all, that their prayers and all their religious
observance are just filled with self and pride. In Isaiah
29:21, when the people are charged with "depriving
the innocent of justice," God's conclusion is that "these
people come near to me with their mouth and honor
me with their lips, but their hearts are far from me."

What Did Jesus Say About Justice?

Jesus's criticism of the religious leaders in Mark 12 was identical. He said: "Watch out for the teachers of the law. . . . They devour widows' houses and for a show make lengthy prayers. Such men will be punished most severely" (Mark 12:38, 40). Behind their excessive religious observances are lives that are insensitive to the vulnerable classes. In Jesus's view, this revealed that they did not know God or his grace at all.[53]

The echoes of the prophets' preaching became even clearer in Luke 11:38–42, where Jesus turned his gaze on the Pharisees, whom he describes as "full of greed and wickedness" (verse 38). They were very religious but they "neglect *justice* and the love of God" (verse 42).[54] Like Isaiah, Jesus taught that a lack of concern for the poor is not a minor lapse, but reveals that something is seriously wrong with one's spiritual compass, the heart. He prescribes a startling remedy: "You Pharisees clean the outside of the cup and dish, but inside you are full of greed. . . . Give what is inside to the poor, and everything will be clean for you" (Luke 11:41). The metaphor is striking. Biblical scholar Joel Green explains it this way: "The disposition of one's possessions signifies the disposition of one's heart."[55] The purification of the heart through grace and love for the poor are of a piece; they go together in the theology of Jesus.

Perhaps the passage in Jesus's teaching that is most

directly like Isaiah 1 and 58 is the famous parable of "the Sheep and the Goats" in Matthew 25:31–46. There Jesus compared Judgment Day to the common task of shepherds who had to identify and remove the goats from the flock. On that day, he taught, there will be many people who claim to have believed in him who he will reject. His true sheep, he insisted, have a heart for "the least of these my brethren," which Jesus defined as the hungry, the stranger, the "naked," the sick, and the imprisoned (verses 35–36). If we assume that Jesus was using the term "brethren" in his usual way, to refer to believers, then he was teaching that genuine disciples of Christ will create a new community that does not exclude the poor, the members of other races, or the powerless, and does deal with their needs sacrificially and practically.[56]

Jesus gave us a long list of his disciples' activities. They were to give food and drink to the hungry, which meant emergency relief. But the "strangers" were immigrants and refugees, and they were to get much more than food. They were to be "invited in." They were not merely sent to a shelter but were to be welcomed into the disciples' homes and lives and, it is implied, given advocacy, friendship, and the basics for pursuing a new life in society. Those who were "naked" were likely very close to what we might call the homeless—the poorest of the poor. The disciples were to "clothe" them.

The sick were to be "looked after." The Greek word used for this is *episkopos,* which meant to give oversight and supervision. That meant that the ill and diseased were to be given comprehensive care until they were well. Finally, the disciples were to "visit" prisoners, which meant they were to give them comfort and encouragement. It is a remarkably comprehensive list. This is the kind of community that Jesus said his true disciples would establish. Believers should be opening their homes and purses to each other, drawing even the poorest and most foreign into their homes and community, giving financial aid, medical treatment, shelter, advocacy, active love, support, and friendship.

But there is something even more startling about this discourse of Jesus. Jesus did *not* say that all this done for the poor was a means of getting salvation, but rather it was the sign that you already had salvation, that true, saving faith was already present.[57] How does he show that? He tells the sheep, "When you embraced the poor, you embraced me," and to the goats he says, "When you ignored the poor, you ignored me." This meant that one's heart attitude toward the poor reveals one's heart attitude toward Christ. Jesus was saying, "If you had opened up your hearts and lives to them, then I would know you have opened up your hearts and lives to me. If you were closed to them, I know you were closed to me." No heart that loves Christ *can* be cold to the vulnerable and the needy. Why is that? The answer for that must wait until chapter 5. At this point, we simply recognize the implications. Anyone who has truly been touched by the grace of God will be vigorous in helping the poor.

A Whole Cloth

In both the gospels of Matthew and Luke, Jesus delivers a famous discourse, which is usually called the Sermon on the Mount. For centuries readers have acknowledged the beauty of its high ethical standards. What is not noticed very often is how Jesus weaves into a whole cloth what we would today call private morality and social justice. Along with the well-known prohibitions against sexual lust in the heart, adultery, and divorce there are calls to give to the poor (Matthew 6:1–4) and to refrain from overwork and materialism (Matthew 6:19–24).

In Western society these sets of concerns have often been split off from one another. In fact, each of America's two main political parties has built its platform on one of these sets of ethical prescriptions to the near exclusion of the other. Conservatism stresses the importance of personal morality, especially the importance of traditional sexual mores and hard work, and feels that liberal charges of racism and social injustice are overblown. On the other hand, liberalism stresses social justice, and considers conservative emphases on moral virtue to be prudish and psychologically harmful. Each side, of course, thinks the other side is smug and self-righteous.

It is not only the political parties that fail to reflect this "whole cloth" Biblical agenda. The churches of America are often more controlled by the surrounding political culture than by the spirit of Jesus and the prophets. Conservative churches tend to concentrate on one set of sins, while liberal ones concentrate on another set. Jesus, like the Old Testament prophets, does not see two categories of morality. In Amos 2:7, we read, "They trample the heads of the poor; father and son go in to the same girl." The prophet condemns social injustice and sexual licentiousness in virtually the same breath (cf. Isaiah 5:8ff). Such denunciations cut across all current conventional political agendas. The Biblical perspective sees sexual immorality and material selfishness as both flowing from self-centeredness rather than God-centeredness.

Raymond Fung, an evangelist in Hong Kong, tells of how he was speaking to a textile worker about the Christian faith, and he urged him to come and visit a church. The man could not go to a service on Sunday without losing a day's wages, but he did so. After the service Fung and the man went to lunch. The worker said, "Well, the sermon hit me." It had been about sin. "What the preacher said was true of me—laziness, a violent temper, and addiction to cheap entertainment." Fung held his breath, trying to control his excitement. Had the gospel message gotten through? He was disappointed. "Nothing was said about my boss," the man said to Fung. When the preacher had gone through the list of sins, he had said, "Nothing about how he employs child laborers, how he doesn't give us the legally required holidays, how he puts on false labels, how he forces us to do overtime. . . ." Fung knew that members of the management class were sitting in the congregation, but those sins were never mentioned. The textile worker agreed that he was a sinner, but he rejected the message of the church because he sensed its incompleteness. Harvie Conn, who related this story in one of his books, added that gospel preaching that targets some sins but not the sins of oppression "cannot possibly work among the overwhelming majority of people in the world, poor peasants and workers."[58]

Jesus's New Community

The early church responded to Jesus's calls for justice and mercy. The apostle Paul viewed ministry to the poor as so important that it was one of the last things he admonished the Ephesian church to do before he left them for the last time. In his farewell address, Paul was able to ground this duty in the teaching of Jesus. "We must help the poor," he said, "remembering the words the Lord Jesus himself said, 'It is more blessed to give than to receive'" (Acts 20:35). You don't use your "last words" without saying something that is all-important to you. For Paul it was: "Don't only preach—help the poor."

Though the church was no longer a nation-state like Israel, the New Testament writers recognized the concern for justice and mercy in the Mosaic legislation and applied it to the church community in a variety of ways. Many Mosaic laws worked toward diminishing the great gap that tends to grow between rich and poor. From the law of "Jubilee" (Leviticus 25) to the rules for gathering manna in Exodus 16, the principle was to increase "equality." When Paul wrote the Corinthian church to ask for an offering to relieve starving Christians in Palestine, he quoted Exodus 16:18 and then said, "At the present time your plenty will supply what they need, so that in turn their plenty will supply what you need. Then there will be equality" (2 Corinthians 8:14).

The New Testament book of James contains some of the most severe condemnation of those who keep their wealth to themselves. James says to the rich: "You have hoarded wealth in the last days. . . . Look!

The wages you failed to pay the workmen who mowed your fields are crying out against you. The cries of the harvesters have reached the ears of the Lord Almighty. You have lived on earth in luxury and self-indulgence" (James 5:1–6). This call could have been lifted right from Isaiah, Jeremiah, or Amos.

No Needy among Them

The book of Acts gives us the most extensive look at the how the early Christians lived their lives together. The very earliest glimpse is in Acts 2:42–47. The gift of the Spirit is given in Acts 2:38, and what results is *koinonia*—a well-known Greek word that is usually translated "fellowship." However, the meaning of the word is unpacked in verses 44–45: "All the believers were together and had everything in common. Selling their possessions and goods, they gave to anyone who had need." Since there were three thousand initial converts, according to Acts 2:41, it almost certainly does not mean they formed a commune and actually shared living quarters. Later, in Acts 4, we are told that those believers with more in the way of wealth and possessions frequently liquidated them and gave the cash to the apostles, who then distributed it to those members of the community who were poor (Acts 4:34–37). Because of this radical generosity,

*there were no needy persons among them. For from
time to time those who owned lands or houses sold
them, brought the money from the sales, and put it
at the apostles' feet, and it was distributed to anyone as he had need.*

Acts 4:34–35[59]

This statement is more significant than it looks. Remember the key Old Testament text, Deuteronomy 15,
in which God declared that if his people obeyed him as
they should, no permanent poverty could exist in their
midst. "There should be no poor among you" (Deuteronomy 15:4). This was the pinnacle of the "social
righteousness" legislation of the Old Testament, which
expressed God's love for the vulnerable and his zeal
to see poverty and want eliminated. It is remarkable,
then, that Acts 4:34 is a direct quote from Deuteronomy 15:4. "It cannot be accidental that Luke, in his
portrayal of the beginnings of the . . . community of
the Holy Spirit, chose to describe them in words taken
almost directly from [Deuteronomy 15:4]."[60] In Deuteronomy, believers were called to open their hands to
the needy as far as there was need, until they were self-
sufficient. The New Testament calls Christians to do
the same (1 John 3:16–17; cf. Deuteronomy 15:7–8).

Acts gives us more insight into the love and justice of the early church. Just as in the Old Testament

a special class of officials was set apart to help with the needy—priests and Levites—so in the New Testament, some were set apart for the same work. The church in Jerusalem conducted a ministry called the "daily *diakonia*" (Acts 6:1). This was a daily distribution of food and other resources to poor widows who were fully supported by the church. This ministry grew until it became too big and complicated for the elders to administer, so they set apart a new group to lead it. Later in the epistles of Paul, those leading this ministry are called "deacons" (Philippians 1:1; 1 Timothy 3:8–13). The Greek word *diakonia* came to mean "humble service to practical needs" in the New Testament, and "diaconal ministry" was a crucial part of the community life of the early church.

But while Christians are to definitely care for the material needs of their brothers and sisters within the Christian community, are they under obligation to care for their poor neighbors, the poor of the world? It is true that the social legislation of the Old Testament is largely about caring for the needy inside the believing community. Also most examples of generosity in the New Testament are of care for the poor within the church, such as the support for widows (Acts 6:1–7; 1 Timothy 5:3–16). Even Jesus's parable of the Sheep and the Goats uses the test of caring for those whom Jesus calls "the least of these my brothers," probably referring to poor believers. Some of this is common sense. Our first responsibility is to our own families and relations (1 Timothy 5:8), and our second responsibility is to other members of the community of faith (Galatians 6:10).

However, the Bible is clear that Christians' practical love, their generous justice, is not to be confined to only those who believe as we do. Galatians 6:10 strikes the balance when Paul says: "Do good to all people, especially the family of faith." Helping "all people" is not optional, it is a command. We don't have to look only to the New Testament to learn this. One of the four vulnerable classes protected by the Hebrew prophets was that of the immigrant. While foreigners residing in Israel could convert, the injunction to provide them with shelter and guard their legal rights was not qualified by whether they had entered the covenant or not. That showed that Israel's justice and compassion was not to be confined to only its own believing community.

But the most famous and powerful statement of Jesus on what it means to love our neighbor is found in his parable of the Good Samaritan (Luke 10:25–37). That important teaching deserves a chapter of its own.[61]

JUSTICE AND
YOUR NEIGHBOR

*Which of these three do you think was a neighbor to
the man who fell into the hands of the robbers?*

Luke 10:36

Who Is My Neighbor?

The single mother, the woman our deacons were so
frustrated with, was literally our church's neighbor. She rented a small house just a few feet away from
our church property. Even the deacons who were the
most negative about her behavior felt some kind of responsibility to help her. Why? Because one of the main
themes of the Bible is that believers should love their
neighbor. This was part of the Mosaic law (Leviticus
19:18), and its language is cited repeatedly in the New
Testament (Matthew 5:43; 19:19; Romans 13:9; Galatians 5:14; James 2:8). However, the text that most in-

[62]

forms Christians' relationships with their neighbors is the parable of the Good Samaritan.[62]

In Luke 10:25 an expert in Biblical law stood up in public and asked Jesus a question. Luke tells us that the law expert wanted to put Jesus to the test, to trap him. Perhaps he had seen how so many irreligious people flocked around Jesus (Luke 15:1–2), people who did not diligently obey the law in every facet of their lives, as did the Pharisees and other religious leaders. The man may have been thinking something like this: "Here is a false teacher who shows little respect for the necessity of obeying the law of God!" So he asked Jesus, "What must I do to inherit eternal life?" He may have expected Jesus to say something like, "Oh, you only have to believe in me," or some other statement that would reveal him to be unconcerned with full obedience to God's Word.

Jesus, however, responded by asking the man a question. "What is written in the law?" The only way to answer such a question is either to spend a week reciting the whole body of Mosaic regulations, or to give a summary of them. The man took Jesus to mean the latter. It was commonly understood that the entire Biblical moral code could be summarized as two master commandments—to love God with all the heart, soul, strength, and mind, and to love one's neighbor as oneself. The law expert recited these. "That's right,"

Jesus replied. "Do them, *and you will live*." Just obey those two commands fully, Jesus said, and you will have eternal life.

It was a brilliant move. One of the problems with moralism—the idea that you can merit God's salvation by your good works and moral efforts—is that it is profoundly hypocritical. It cannot live up to its own standards. The Pharisees concentrated on complying with the legal details of God's law. "You tithe mint, dill, and cummin," Jesus once said to the religious leaders (Matthew 23:23). That is, in seeking to obey God's law to give away a tenth of all their income, they were careful to even tithe 10 percent of the cooking herbs out of their garden. By devoting themselves to this level of diligence, they comforted themselves that they were keeping themselves acceptable to God.

But here Jesus beats them at their own game. In effect Jesus's message was something like this: "Have you actually looked at the kind of righteous life that all these specific laws are really after? Have you seen what kind of life God really wants from you? Do you love God with every fiber of your being every minute of the day? Do you meet the needs of your neighbor with all the joy, energy, and fastidiousness with which you meet your own needs? *That* is the kind of life you owe your God and your fellow human beings. God created you and sustains your life every second. He has given you everything and therefore it is only fair that you give him everything. If you can give God a life like that, you will certainly merit eternal life."

This was, of course, an impossibly high standard, but that was the point. Jesus was showing the man the perfect righteousness the law demanded so that he could see that he was ultimately powerless to fulfill it. To use other language, he was seeking to convict the man of sin, of the impossibility of self-salvation, by using against him the very law he knew so much about. Jesus said in effect: "My friend, I do take the law seriously, even more seriously than you do. If you can do what it commands, you will live." He was seeking to humble the man. Why? It is only if we truly see the love God requires in his law that we will be willing and able to receive the love God offers in his gospel of free salvation through Jesus. Jesus was encouraging the man to seek the grace of God.

The law expert is shaken by Jesus's move. The text tells us "he wanted to justify himself" (verse 29), which, of course, is what Jesus had discerned about his heart already. But Jesus's first effort was not enough to put him off his self-justification project. Though he felt the weight of Jesus's argument, the man saw another way to defend himself. He countered, "Who *is* my neighbor?"

The implication was clear. "OK, Jesus," he was saying. "Yes, I see that I have to love my neighbor—but what does that really mean, and who does that really mean?" In other words, the law expert wanted to whittle down this command to make it more achievable, and to keep his works-righteousness approach to life intact. "Surely," he implied, "you don't mean I have to love and meet the needs of *every*one!"

The Good Samaritan

In response, Jesus tells the story of the Good Samaritan. A Jewish man was riding through a mountainous, remote area where he was robbed, beaten, and left in the road "half-dead" (verse 30). Along came first a priest and then a Levite, one of the temple workers who assisted the priests. These were both people who should have stopped to give aid, because the Jew was their brother in the faith. However, they "pass by on the other side," possibly because it would have been extremely dangerous to stop on a desolate road in a region infested with highwaymen.

Then a Samaritan came along the road. Samaritans and Jews were the bitterest of enemies. Samaritans were seen by Jews as racial "half-breeds" and religious heretics, and so there was great animosity between them. Yet when the Samaritan saw the man in the road, he was moved with compassion. He braved the danger by stopping, giving him emergency medical aid, and then transporting him to an inn. He then paid the innkeeper and charged him to care for the man until he had fully recuperated. That would have been a substantial expense.

What was Jesus doing with this story? He was giving a radical answer to the question, What does it mean to love your neighbor? What is the definition of "love"? Jesus answered that by depicting a man meeting material, physical, and economic needs through deeds. Caring for people's material and economic needs is not an option for Jesus. He refused to allow the law expert to limit the implications of this command to love. He said it meant being sacrificially involved with the vulnerable, just as the Samaritan risked his life by stopping on the road.

But Jesus refuses to let us limit not only how we love, but who we love. It is typical for us to think of our neighbors as people of the same social class and means (cf. Luke 14:12). We instinctively tend to limit for whom we exert ourselves. We do it for people like us, and for people whom we like. Jesus will have none of that. By depicting a Samaritan helping a Jew, Jesus could not have found a more forceful way to say that anyone at all in need—regardless of race, politics, class, and religion—is your neighbor. Not everyone is your brother or sister in the faith, but everyone is your neighbor, and you must love your neighbor.

Objections to Jesus

I have preached this parable over the years, and it always raises a host of questions and objections, many of which sound like the kind of questions that the law expert would have asked. No one has helped me answer these questions more than Jonathan Edwards, who was minister of the congregational church in Northampton, Massachusetts, from 1729 to 1751. Despite how long ago he wrote, both the questions he fielded and the answers he gave are remarkably up-to-date.

Edwards became aware of growing poverty and increasing social stratification in his town.[63] Some of the reasons for this were socioeconomic. By 1730, most of the town's usable land had been parceled out, and it was difficult for newcomers or young families to get an economic foothold. Conflicts grew between creditors and debtors, long-term residents and newcomers, old and young. But Edwards also believed that the reason for the rising tension between the haves and the have-nots was spiritual. In 1733 he preached a sermon entitled "The Duty of Charity to the Poor."[64] The word "neighbor" is found in the sermon nearly sixty times, and the discourse stands as one of the most thorough-going applications of the parable of the Good Samaritan to a body of believers that can be found anywhere.[65] The heart of the sermon is a set of answers to a series of common objections Edwards always heard whenever he preached or spoke about the duty of sharing money and goods with the poor. All of the questions sought to put limits on the Biblical injunction to love their neighbor.

One of the objections was "Though they be needy, yet they are not in extremity. [They are not destitute.]" I remember one of my parishioners responding to one of my sermons in a similar manner. "All the poor people in my part of town have nice TV sets. They aren't starving," he said. But Edwards says that this hardheartedness is not in accord with the Biblical command to love your neighbor as *yourself.* We don't wait until we are in "extremity" before doing something about our condition, he argued, so why should we wait until our neighbor is literally starving before we help?[66] Edwards goes further, and asks if Christians who say this remember that we are to love others as Christ loved us. "The Christian spirit will make us apt to sympathize with our neighbor when we see him under any difficulty . . . we ought to have such a spirit of love to him that we should be afflicted with him in his affliction."[67] Christ literally walked in our shoes and entered into our affliction. Those who will not help others until they are destitute reveal that Christ's love has not yet turned them into the sympathetic persons the gospel should make them.

Another objection comes from people who say they "have nothing to spare" and that they barely have enough for their own needs. But one of the main lessons of the Good Samaritan parable is that real love entails risk and sacrifice. Edwards responds that when you say, "I can't help anyone," you usually mean, "I can't help anyone without burdening myself, cutting in to how I live my life." But, Edwards argues, that's exactly what Biblical love requires. He writes:

We in many cases may, by the rule of the gospel, be obliged to give to others when we can't without suffering ourselves. . . . If our neighbor's difficulties and necessities are much greater than ours and we see that they are not like to be relieved, we should be willing to suffer with them and to take part of their burden upon ourselves. Or else how is that rule fulfilled of bearing one another's burdens? If we are never obliged to relieve others' burdens but only when we can do it without burdening ourselves, then how do we bear our neighbor's burdens, when we bear no burden at all?[68]

Two other objections Edwards takes on are that the poor person "is of a very ill temper; he is of an ungrateful spirit" and "he has brought himself to his [poverty] by his own fault." These are both abiding problems with helping the poor. These objections were behind the deacon's opposition to giving the single mother next door any more aid. We all want to help kindhearted, upright people, whose poverty came upon them through no foolishness or contribution of their own, and who will respond to our aid with gratitude and joy. However, almost no one like that exists. As we saw in chapter 2, the causes of poverty are complex and intertwined. And while it is important that our aid to the poor really helps them and doesn't create dependency, Edwards makes short work of these objections by, again, appealing to the gospel itself.

In dealing with the objection that many of the poor do not have upright, moral characters, he counters that we did not either, and yet Christ put himself out for us:

> Christ loved us, and was kind to us, and was willing to relieve us, though we were very hateful persons, of an evil disposition, not deserving of any good . . . so we should be willing to be kind to those who are . . . very undeserving.[69]

When answering the objection that the poor have often contributed to their condition, Edwards is re-markably balanced yet insistently generous. He points out that it is possible some people simply do not have "a natural faculty to manage affairs to advantage." In other words, some people persistently make sincere but very bad decisions about money and possessions. Ed-wards says we should consider the lack of this faculty to be almost like being born with impaired eyesight:

> Such a faculty is a gift that God bestows on some, and not on others. And it is not owing to themselves. . . . This is as reasonable as that he to whom Providence has imparted sight should be willing to help him to whom sight is denied, and that he should have the benefit of the sight of others, who has none of his own. . . .[70]

But what if their economic plight is more directly the result of selfish, indolent, or violent behavior? As Ed-wards puts it in the language of his time, what if "they are come to want by a vicious idleness and prodigality"? He counters that "we are not thereby excused from all obligation to relieve them, unless they continue in those vices." Then he explains why. Christ found us in the same condition. Our spiritual bankruptcy was due to our own sin, yet he came and gave us what we needed.

The rules of the gospel direct us to forgive them . . . [for] Christ hath loved us, pitied us, and greatly laid out himself to relieve us from that want and misery which we brought on ourselves by our own folly and wickedness. We foolishly and perversely threw away those riches with which we were provided, upon which we might have lived and been happy to all eternity.[71]

At this point, the listener may discern a loophole. Edwards says that we should not continue to aid a poor person if that person continues to act "viciously" and to persist in the same behavior. Yet Edwards has a final blow to strike. What about the rest of the person's family? Sometimes, he says, we will need to give aid to families even when the parents act irresponsibly, for the children's sake. "If they continue in the same courses still, yet . . . if we can't relieve those of their families without them having something of it, yet that ought not to be a bar in the way of our charity."[72]

Using this argument of Edwards, I got our deacons to continue their aid to the single mother. As time went on it became clearer to the deacons that the reason she had squandered the church's money on restaurants and new bikes was that she felt terribly guilty for the poor life she was giving her kids. "It's so hard being the child of a single mom in this town. And I can't buy them the nice things other kids get." When she had the church's money in hand, she could not resist the temptation to take the children out to restaurants and buy them bikes, because it made her children feel like they were now part of a normal family.

When we began to look at her in this light, her behavior not only made more sense, but our hearts were touched. Her actions were not simply selfish. Nevertheless, she had not kept her word to us, and we showed her that what she had done was shortsighted. She needed to get out from under her most urgent debts, like utility bills, rent, and medical fees. Then she needed to have a plan to acquire better skills and a better job. To give her children a better life she needed a plan and the discipline to carry it out. We were willing to help her with that longer-term plan if she would work with us responsibly in the near term. The deacons recognized, however, that her children needed a lot of support. They needed "big brothers" and "big sisters," tutors and mentors who did not steal their love from their mother but strengthened their respect for her. In other words, this family needed much more than a financial subsidy.

She agreed to work with the deacons, and over a longer period of time, the family's life began to improve. Without the Good Samaritan parable, and the thorough, thoughtful application of its principles by

Jonathan Edwards, we would have missed this whole opportunity. We might have said, "When you talk about loving our neighbor, you can't mean someone like her, can you?"

The Great Samaritan

One of the remarkable "twists" that Jesus gave to his parable was the placement of the Jewish man in the story. Remember that Jesus was telling this story to a Jewish man, the law expert. What if Jesus had told the parable like this?

> A Samaritan was beaten up and left half dead in a road. Then a Jewish man came along the road. He saw him and had compassion on him and ministered to him.

How would the law expert and his Jewish hearers have responded? They most likely would have said, "This is a ridiculous story! No self-respecting Jew would ever do such a thing. This is just what I suspected. You make unrealistic, outrageous demands on people."

But instead, Jesus put a Jew in the road as the victim. In other words, he was asking each listener to imagine himself to be a victim of violence, dying, with no hope if this Samaritan did not stop and help. How would you want the Samaritan to act if that was your situation? Wouldn't you want him to be a neighbor to you, across all racial and religious barriers? Of course you would. Jesus was saying something like this:

What if your only hope was to get ministry from someone who not only did not owe you any help—but who actually owed you the opposite? What if your only hope was to get free grace from someone who had every justification, based on your relationship to him, to trample you?

And so Jesus ended the story with a question: "Who was the neighbor to the man in the road?" The law expert must admit that it was "the one who showed mercy" (verse 37). He had to agree that, if he had been the needy man in the road, and had been offered neighbor-love from someone from whom he would have expected rejection, he would have nonetheless accepted it. It was only then that Jesus says: "Go and do likewise." He had made his case, and the law expert had no rejoinder. Your neighbor is anyone in need.

But the law expert did not have the vantage point to see what we can see. According to the Bible, we are all like that man, dying in the road. Spiritually, we are "dead in trespasses and sins" (Ephesians 2:5). But when Jesus came into our dangerous world, he came down our road. And though we had been his enemies, he was moved with compassion by our plight (Romans 5:10). He came to us and saved us, not merely at the risk of his life, as in the case of the Samaritan, but at the cost of his life. On the cross he paid a debt we could never have paid ourselves. Jesus is the Great Samaritan to whom the Good Samaritan points.

Before you can give this neighbor-love, you need to receive it. Only if you see that you have been saved graciously by someone who owes you the opposite will you go out into the world looking to help absolutely anyone in need. Once we receive this ultimate, radical neighbor-love through Jesus, we can start to be the neighbors that the Bible calls us to be.

FIVE

WHY SHOULD WE
DO JUSTICE?

*Suppose a brother or sister is without clothes and daily
food. If one of you says, "Go, I wish you well; keep
warm and well fed," but does nothing about his physical needs, what good is it? In the same way, faith by
itself, if it is not accompanied by action, is dead.*

James 2:15–17

Our family moved to Manhattan in 1989 to plant
a new church, Redeemer Presbyterian. Because
it was a brand-new church in a very secular place, many
of the people who came into our congregation had
little in the way of church background. One woman
who was very prosperous discovered that her new faith
brought with it many new, hitherto unthinkable ideas
about race and class. Specifically, she realized that she
now had more in common with Christians who were
poor than she did with many others of her own so-

cial class. In fact, she recognized in poor believers a love for God and a wisdom that she considered often superior to her own. Any sense of superiority or even paternalistic pity toward the poor began to fade away.

What was going on? The experience of the grace through the gospel of Jesus was changing this woman's attitudes and motivation, even before she came into any contact with the ethical injunctions to give to the poor. It is to this all-important subject we turn in this chapter.

The Importance of Motivation

You could make a good argument that our problem in society today is not that people don't know they should share with others and help the poor. Most people do know and believe this. The real problem is that, while knowing it, they are insufficiently motivated to actually do it. Therefore, there is no greater question than how to motivate people to do what they ought for the hungry and poor of the world. Arthur Leff, former professor at Yale Law School, wrote:

> Looking around the world, it appears that if all men are brothers, the ruling model is Cain and Abel. Neither reason, nor love, nor even terror, seems to have worked to make us "good," and worse than that, there is no reason why anything should.[73]

Leff chalks up our failure not to the fact we don't know what is right to do—we do—but to the lack of a sufficient, driving motivation to do it. One of the concerns of Leff's essay is that we now live in a relativistic age, in which it is virtually impossible to convince people that there is an absolute moral standard that they must bow to, whether they like it or not. So to get people to be just and generous we appeal to love, or to practical reason. For example, we argue: "Don't you see that it is eminently practical to honor human rights, to care about the environment, to generously direct resources toward the poor, to live peaceably with those of different races, religions, and nationalities? The world will be such a better place for everyone if we all do this!" But nothing has worked, he concludes.

I think Leff is correct, that appeals to love and mercy do not work any more than appeals to reason. If so, philosopher Richard Rorty is wrong in his analysis. In "Human Rights, Rationality, and Sentimentality" he agrees with Leff and others that we now live in a relativistic age, in which no one has any right to say there are moral absolutes. Rorty writes that, to the question "Why should I care about a stranger, a person who is no kin to me, a person whose habits I find disgusting?" the older answer was "Because you have a *moral obligation* to her." We can no longer give that answer in our society, Rorty argues, because who is to say what the universal moral obligations are? Instead, Rorty says:

> A better sort of answer is the sort of long, sad, sentimental story which begins "Because this is what it is like to be in her situation—to be far from home, among strangers," or "Because she might become your daughter-in-law," or "Because her mother would grieve for her." Such stories, repeated and varied over the centuries, have induced us, the rich, safe, powerful, people, to tolerate, and even to cherish, powerless people— people whose appearance or habits or beliefs at first seemed an insult to our own moral identity, our sense of the limits of permissible human variation.[74]

Leff, for his part, disagrees, and with good cause. Was it sad, sentimental stories that ended apartheid in South Africa or segregation in the South, or was it very direct political action? Do we think more sad, sentimental stories could change the views of the Serbs toward Bosnians, and vice versa?

Now we can see what an important and powerful resource the Bible gives us when it provides not merely the bare ethical obligation for doing justice, but a revolutionary new inner power and dynamism to do so. The Bible gives believers two basic motivations—joyful awe before the goodness of God's creation, and the experience of God's grace in redemption.

Honoring the Image

One Biblical motivation for doing justice is to look to the beginning of the Bible, to the creation, where Genesis 1:26–27 tells us: "So God created man in his own image." What does being an "image" mean? It conveys the idea of being a work of art or of great craftsmanship. Human beings are not accidents, but creations. Without a belief in creation, we are forced to face the implication that ultimately there is no good reason to treat human beings as having dignity. Chief Justice Oliver Wendell Holmes, Jr., said it well when he wrote:

> When one thinks coldly I see no reason for attributing to man a significance different in kind from that which belongs to a baboon or a grain of sand.[75]

Contrast this with the implications of the Biblical view of humanity, made in the image of God, made to live with God for eternity. C. S. Lewis writes:

Why Should We Do Justice?

There are no *ordinary* people. You have never talked to a mere mortal. Nations, cultures, arts, civilizations—these are mortal, and their life is to ours as the life of a gnat. It is immortals whom we joke with, work with, marry, snub, and exploit. . . .[76]

The word "image" also can mean "to resemble," as a child resembles a parent, or "to represent," as a mirror reflects and represents an object. A mirror can't depict an object in all its dimensions, yet the image upon it is a true likeness. What is it about us that resembles or reflects God? Over the years thinkers have pointed to human rationality, personality, and creativity, or to our moral and aesthetic sense and our deep need for and ability to give love in relationships. All of this and much more goes into being the image of God, though we must beware of trying to nail it down into a list.

The Bible teaches that the sacredness of God has in some ways been imparted to humanity, so that every human life is sacred and every human being has dignity. When God put his image upon us, we became beings of infinite, inestimable value. In Genesis 9:5–6, we read the reason that God considered murder to be so heinous. "For your lifeblood I will surely demand an accounting," he said, ". . . for in his own image God has made man." In James 3:9, the writer castigates sharp-tongued people. It is a considerably less serious evil than murder, and yet he forbids all verbal abuse because such miscreants "curse men, who have been made in God's likeness." There is something so valuable about human beings that not only may they not be murdered, but they can't even be cursed without failing to give them their due, based on the worth bestowed upon them by God. The image of God carries with it the right to not be mistreated or harmed.

All human beings have this right, this worth, according to the Bible. Notice that neither Genesis nor James limits the prohibition on abusive behavior to "good" people. Regardless of their record or character, all human beings have an irreducible glory and significance to them, because God loves them, indeed, he "loves all that he has made" (Psalms 145:9, 17). He loves even those who turn away from him (Ezekiel 33:11; John 3:16).[77] This bestows a worth on them. Nicholas Wolterstorff gives us an example of how this works. He imagines some foreigner, knowing nothing about U.S. history, becoming perplexed to find that the Mount Vernon estate in Virginia is preserved as a national monument and treated as an object of such great worth. After all, she might observe, there are quite a number of old Virginia plantation houses of much greater architectural merit and beauty than Mount Vernon. We would respond that this was the house of

George Washington, the founder of our country, and that explains it. The internal merits and quality of the house are irrelevant. Because we treasure the owner, we honor his house.[78] Because it was precious to him, and we revere him, it is precious to us. So we must treasure each and every human being as a way of showing due respect for the majesty of their owner and Creator.

The Image of God and Civil Rights

I'm not sure that we understand what a radical notion this is. Aristotle said famously that some people are born to be slaves. Why did he think that? Aristotle and other Greek philosophers believed that the dignity of human beings resided in certain capacities, in particular, rationality. In their view, rational beings had dignity and rights worthy of respect, but not all human beings were equally rational. Aristotle wrote:

. . . [H]e who participates in rational principle enough to apprehend, but not to have, such a principle, is a slave by nature. Whereas the lower animals cannot even apprehend a [rational] principle; they obey their instincts. . . . Nature would like to distinguish between the bodies of freemen and slaves, making the one strong for servile labor, the other upright, and although useless for such services, useful for political life in the arts both of war and peace. . . . It is clear, then, that some men are by nature free, and others slaves, and that for these latter slavery is both expedient and right.[79]

Aristotle was merely reflecting our natural intuitions. Does our actual experience of life lead us to believe that every human being is equally valuable and has equal dignity? No. The default mode of the human heart is to label some people "barbarians." We still do it today, but in ancient times, it was just common sense that some kinds of people had dignity and deserved respect while others did not at all.

The doctrine of the image of God, however, allows no such distinctions. A recent book by Richard Wayne Wills, *Martin Luther King, Jr., and the Image of God* (Oxford, 2009), makes the case that the doctrine of the image of God was at the very heart of the Civil Rights Movement. In a sermon entitled "The American Dream," Martin Luther King, Jr., said:

You see, the founding fathers were really influenced by the Bible. The whole concept of the *imago dei*, as it is expressed in Latin, the "image of God," is the idea that all men have something within them that God injected. Not that they have substantial unity with God, but that every man has a capacity to have fellowship with God. And this gives him a uniqueness, it gives him worth, it gives him dignity. And we must never forget this as a nation: There are no gradations in the image of God. Every man from a treble white to a bass black is significant on God's keyboard, precisely because every man is made in the image of God. One day we will learn that. We will know one day that God made us to live together as brothers and to respect the dignity and worth of every man. This is why we must fight segregation with all of our nonviolent might.[80]

The image of God, then, is the first great motivation for living lives of generous justice, serving the needs and guarding the rights of those around us. It brings humility before the greatness of each human being made and loved by God. C. S. Lewis expressed it this way:

The load, or weight, or burden of my neighbor's glory should be laid daily on my back, a load so heavy that only humility can carry it, and the backs of the proud will be broken. . . . This does not mean that we are to be perpetually solemn. We must play. But our merriment must be of that kind (and it is, in fact, the merriest kind) which exists between people who have, from the outset, taken each other seriously—no flippancy, no superiority, no presumption. And our charity must be a real and costly love, with deep feeling for the sins in spite of which we love the sinner—no mere tolerance or indulgence which parodies love as flippancy parodies merriment. . . .[81]

Recognizing God's Ownership

There is another important way in which the doctrine of creation motivates Christians toward sharing their resources with others. If God is the Creator and author of all things, that means everything we have in life belongs to God.

In Genesis 1, God gives Adam and Eve "dominion" over the creation. This was a call to leadership, but it was also a call to stewardship. God made Adam and Eve "rulers over the works of [God's] hands" (Psalms 8:8) but "the earth is the Lord's, and everything in it" (Psalms 24:1). In other words, God gave humanity authority over the world's resources but not ownership. We have received what we have in the way a fund manager receives other people's money to invest, or as, in ancient times, the steward of an estate received his authority over the estate. The steward of a great estate lived comfortably and enjoyed the fruits of his labor, but he never made the mistake of thinking that the wealth under his care was all his. He was tasked to manage it in a way that pleased the owner and was fair to his fellow servants.

This concept is counterintuitive for most Americans. We believe that if we have had success in life, it is mainly the result of our own hard work, and we therefore have an absolute right to use our money as we see fit. But while the Bible agrees industriousness or the lack of it is an irreplaceable part of why you are successful or not (Proverbs 6:9–11; 10:4), it is never the main reason. If you had been born on a mountaintop in Tibet in the thirteenth century, instead of a Western country in the twentieth century, then no matter how hard you worked, you wouldn't have had much to show for it. If you have money, power, and status today, it is due to the century and place in which you were born, to your talents and capacities and health, none of which you earned. In short, all your resources are in the end the gift of God. That is why David, the wealthiest man in Israel, prayed:

> *Yours, O LORD, is the greatness and the power and the glory and the majesty and the splendor, for everything in heaven and earth is yours. . . . Wealth and honor come from you; you are the ruler of all*

things. In your hands are strength and power to ex-
alt and give strength to all. . . . But who am I, and
who are my people, that we should be able to give as
generously as this? Everything comes from you, and
we have given you only what comes from your hand.

1 Chronicles 29:11–14

Because David understood this principle—that ultimately all we have is a gift of God—he does not view
his wealth as fully his own. Old Testament scholar
Bruce Waltke concludes, after studying both the word
mishpat and its kindred word *tzadeqah* (righteousness), that in the Old Testament

the righteous [*tzaddiq*] . . . are willing to disadvantage themselves to advantage the community;
the wicked are willing to disadvantage the community to advantage themselves.[82]

Therefore, just men and women see their money
as belonging in some ways to the entire human community around them, while the unjust or unrighteous
see their money as strictly theirs and no one else's. After all, they earned it, and that's the main reason they
have it. That view of life is naïve, as we have seen, and
it collides head-on with the Bible. So in Deuteronomy
24 we read:

Why Should We Do Justice?

*When you are harvesting your field and you over-
look a sheaf, do not go back and get it. It is for the
immigrant, the fatherless, and the widow. . . .*

Deuteronomy 24:14,17,19

The reference to the harvest was an exhortation to
landowners to allow the poor to "glean." If we read
this text closely, we see that part of the landowner's
harvest was "for" the immigrant and poor. That means
that in God's eyes, it was actually *theirs*.[83] We should
be careful not to think this means that the land belonged to the poor—it belonged ultimately to God
and provisionally to the landowner. In God's view,
however, while the poor did not have a right to the
ownership of the farmer's land, they had a right to some
of its produce. If the owner did not limit his profits
and provide the poor with an opportunity to work for
their own benefit in the fields, he did not simply deprive the poor of charity but of justice, of their right.
Why? A lack of generosity refuses to acknowledge that
your assets are not really yours, but God's.

Here is another example. Think of the millions of
children and teenagers in this country who have grown
up in poverty. They attend failing schools and live in
an environment unconducive to reading and learning.
By the time they are in their teens many of them are
functionally illiterate. This locks them into poverty

or worse. It is estimated that a majority of convicts in prison are illiterate. Who is to blame?

Conservatives may argue that this is the parents' fault. It is due to a failure of moral character and the breakdown of the family. Liberals, however, see it as a failure of government to stem systemic racism and to change unjust social structures. But nobody says that it is the children's fault they were born where they were. Those children are in poverty largely because they were not born into a family like mine. My three sons, just by being born where they were, have a far better chance to have a flourishing, happy life in society. There is an inequitable distribution of both goods and opportunities in this world. Therefore, if you have been assigned the goods of this world by God and you don't share them with others, it isn't just stinginess, it is injustice.

Responding to God's Grace

As important as the doctrine of creation is, the most frequently cited Biblical motivation for doing justice is the grace of God in redemption. This theme does not just begin in the New Testament. In Deuteronomy, Moses said to the people:

Circumcise your hearts, therefore, and do not be stiff-necked any longer. For the LORD your God

Why Should We Do Justice?

*is God of gods and Lord of lords, the great God,
mighty and awesome, who shows no partiality and
accepts no bribes. He defends the cause of the fatherless and the widow, and loves the alien, giving him
food and clothing. And you are to love those who
are aliens, for you yourselves were aliens in Egypt.*

Deuteronomy 10:16–19

The Israelites had been poor, racial outsiders in
Egypt. How then, Moses asks, could they be callous to
the poor, racial outsiders in their own midst? Through
Moses, God said: "Israel, you were liberated by me.
You did not accomplish it—I performed it *for* you, by
my grace. Now do the same for others. Untie the yoke,
unlock the shackles, feed and clothe them, as I did for
you."[84] Of particular interest is Moses's exhortation to
"circumcise your hearts" (verse 16). Circumcision was
the external sign that a family had come into a covenant
relationship with God. Heart circumcision was a passionate commitment to God on the inside. Meeting the
needs of the orphan, the widow, and the poor immigrant
was a sign that the Israelites' relationship with God was
not just formal and external but internal as well.

The logic is clear. If a person has grasped the meaning of God's grace in his heart, he will do justice. If he
doesn't live justly, then he may say with his lips that
he is grateful for God's grace, but in his heart he is far

from him. If he doesn't care about the poor, it reveals that at best he doesn't understand the grace he has experienced, and at worst he has not really encountered the saving mercy of God. Grace should make you just.

Another example of this reasoning is found in Isaiah 58:2. God sees the Israelites fasting. The only fast commanded by law was for the Day of Atonement, Yom Kippur (Leviticus 23:26–32). All during the year the Israelites were to obey the moral law diligently, but God knew that this was not something that they would ever do satisfactorily or sufficiently. Our sins create a barrier between God and us, but by his grace the Lord makes a provision for sin. So once a year the high priest entered the sanctuary of the tabernacle and offered a blood sacrifice, atoning for the sins of the people. The Day of Atonement meant that God's relationship with his people was based on grace and forgiveness. That was why fasting was an appropriate way to observe Yom Kippur. By abstaining from pleasures, particularly food, they exhibited humility before God and showed they believed in the basic message of Yom Kippur, namely, that we are all sinners saved by grace.

But God was deeply displeased with the Israelites' fasting:

Why have we fasted," they say, "and you have not seen it? Why have we humbled ourselves, and you

have not noticed?" "Yet on the day of your fasting,
you do as you please and exploit all your workers. . . .
Is this the kind of fast I have chosen, only a day for
a man to humble himself? Is it only for bowing one's
head like a reed and for lying on sackcloth and
ashes? Is that what you call a fast, a day acceptable
to the LORD?"

Isaiah 58:3–5

God sees economically comfortable people abstaining from food, "going without" for a day or two,
but not being willing to abstain from exploiting their
workers. Though they demonstrate the external sign
of belief in grace—fasting—their lives reveal that their
hearts have not been changed.

Is not this the kind of fasting I have chosen: to loose
the chains of injustice and untie the cords of the
yoke, to set the oppressed free and break every yoke?
Is it not to share your food with the hungry and to
provide the poor wanderer with shelter—when you
see the naked, to clothe him, and not to turn away
from your own flesh and blood?

Isaiah 58:3,5–7

Fasting should be a symbol of a pervasive change
across the whole face of one's life. People changed by

grace should go, as it were, on a permanent fast. Self-indulgence and materialism should be given up and replaced by a sacrificial lifestyle of giving to those in need. They should spend not only their money but "themselves" (verse 10) on others. What is this permanent fasting? It is to work against injustice, to share food, clothing, and home with the hungry and the homeless. That is the real proof that you believe your sins have been atoned for, and that you have truly been humbled by that knowledge and are now living a life submitted to God and shaped by knowledge of him. People who fast and pray ritually but still show pride and haughtiness toward the poor and needy reveal that no true humbling has ever penetrated their hearts. If you look down at the poor and stay aloof from their suffering, you have not really understood or experienced God's grace.

It is difficult not to think of the elder brother in Jesus's parable of the prodigal son. The people God addresses, like the elder brother, complain that God is not doing their will, and that they deserve his support since they have been so obedient. But the truth is that their obedience is only formal and external; it is filled with self-righteousness and is motivated by a desire to control God, not actually serve him. Such people show they are complying with religious observances as a way of "getting ahead" with God and others. This deadly spiritual condition shows itself in a lack of loving service toward others, and particularly an indifference to the poor.

Justification and Justice

Is the reasoning of the New Testament any different? No, not at all. One of the main themes of the writings of Paul is justification by faith. Many religions teach that if you live as you ought, then God will accept and bless you. But Paul taught that if you receive God's acceptance and blessing as a free gift through Jesus Christ, then you can and will live as you ought. During the Reformation, reformers like Martin Luther and John Calvin rediscovered and restated this doctrine. Though we deserve the wrath of God and punishment for our sin, Jesus Christ came and stood in our place. He lived the life we should have lived and therefore earned the blessing of salvation that such a perfect life deserves. But at the end he died on the cross and took the curse that our imperfect lives deserve. When we repent and believe in Jesus, all the punishment we are due is taken away, having been borne by him, and all the honor he is due for his righteous life and death is given to us. We are now loved and treated by God as if we had done all the great things that Jesus did.[85] Martin Luther gave this teaching a classic, bold expression in the preface to his commentary on the Galatians:

There is a righteousness which Paul calls "the righteousness of faith." God imputes it to us apart from our works. . . . [Now] though I am a sinner in myself, with regard to the moral law, . . . yet in that righteousness I have no sin, no sting of conscience, no fear of death. I have another righteousness and life above this life, which is Christ the Son of God.[86]

When we come to the New Testament book of James, we find what at first appears to be a contradiction of Paul, who wrote that Christians are "justified freely by his grace" (Romans 3:24) and "justified by faith apart from observing the law . . . apart from works" (Romans 3:28; 4:6). But James says:

What good is it, my brothers, if a man claims to have faith but does not have works? Can that faith save him? . . . So faith by itself, if it does not have works, is dead.

James 2:14,17

The contradiction is only apparent. While a sinner can get into relationship with God by only faith (Paul), the ultimate proof that you have saving faith is the changed life that true faith inevitably produces (James).[87] To bring Paul's and James's teaching together, we can say: "We are saved by faith alone, but not by a faith that remains alone. True faith will always produce a changed life."

However, James does not merely say that true faith will change one's life in general. He goes on to describe the "works" that he says always accompany a living, justifying faith.

> *Suppose a brother or sister is without clothes and daily food. If one of you says to him, "Go, I wish you well; keep warm and well fed," but does nothing about his physical needs, what good is it? In the same way, faith by itself, if it is not accompanied by action, is dead.*
>
> James 2:15–16

If you look at someone without adequate resources and do nothing about it, James teaches, your faith is "dead," it is not really saving faith. So what are the "works" he is talking about? He is saying that a life poured out in deeds of service to the poor is the inevitable sign of any real, true, justifying, gospel-faith. Grace makes you just. If you are not just, you've not truly been justified by faith.

Justification is the doctrine that God has *not* given us our "just deserts." Why, then, would the doctrine and experience of justification lead a person to become more involved in doing justice?

A Higher View of the Law

Let's think for a moment about the alternatives to the doctrine of justification by faith. Some people believe that if human beings try hard enough to obey God they can be saved. But believing that is to have an understanding of the law that is a much "lower bar." Jesus raised the bar infinitely when he said, "You've heard it said, 'Do not kill' . . . but I say to you anyone who is angry with his brother . . . who says to his brother, 'You fool' . . . will be in danger of the fire of hell" (Matthew 5:21–22). The view that we can only be justified by grace rests in a very high view of the demands of God's law. Why can we never be saved by our own moral efforts? It is because the law of God is so magnificent, just, and demanding that we could never fulfill it.

There are other people who believe that God is not really alienated from the human race because of our sin. In this view, all Jesus did on the cross was to exhibit God's love for us. There was no punishment to be taken or penalty to be paid. There was no "divine wrath" to be appeased. But again, in this view we have a much lower view of God's law. The classic Christian doctrine is that on the cross Jesus actually saved us by standing in our place and paying our debt to the law of God. If the Lord takes his law so seriously that he could not shrug off our disobedience to it, that he *had* to become human, come to earth, and die a terrible death—then we must take that law very seriously too. The law of God demands equity and justice, and love of one's neighbor. People who believe strongly in the doctrine of justification by faith alone will have this high regard for God's law and justice. They will be passionate about seeing God's justice honored in the world.

A New Attitude toward the Poor

At the beginning of the chapter I recounted the experience of a prosperous woman who, after finding faith in Christ, discovered that any sense of superiority toward the poor was swept away. In the introduction I mentioned my friend Easley, who discovered that the doctrine of justification opened his eyes to his own racism. How does this happen?

Jesus said, "Blessed are the poor *in spirit*" (Matthew 5:3), and most scholars over the centuries have understood that God's blessing and salvation come to those who "acknowledge spiritual bankruptcy."[88] It means to see that you are deeply in debt before God, and you have no ability to even begin to redeem your-self. God's free generosity to you, at infinite cost to him, was the only thing that saved you. What if, how-ever, you aren't poor in spirit? That would mean you don't believe you are so sinful, morally bankrupt, and lost that only free grace can possibly save you. You may find the classic Christian doctrines about hu-manity's deep sin and lostness to be too harsh. On the contrary, you believe that God owes you some things—he ought to answer your prayers and to bless you for the many good things you've done. Even though the Bible doesn't use the term, by inference we can say that you are "middle-class in spirit." You feel that you've earned a certain standing with God through your hard work. You also may believe, as we noted in the last chapter, that the success and the re-sources you have are primarily due to your own indus-try and energy.

My experience as a pastor has been that those who are middle-class in spirit tend to be indifferent to the poor, but people who come to grasp the gospel of grace and become spiritually poor find their hearts gravitat-ing toward the materially poor. To the degree that the gospel shapes your self-image, you will identify with those in need. You will see their tattered clothes and think: "All my righteousness is a filthy rag, but in Christ we can be clothed in his robes of righteousness." When you come upon those who are economically poor, you cannot say to them, "Pull yourself up by your bootstraps!" because you certainly did not do that spiritually. Jesus intervened for you. And you cannot say, "I won't help you because you got yourself into this mess," since God came to earth, moved into your spiritually poor neighborhood, as it were, and helped you even though your spiritual problems were your own fault. In other words, when Christians who understand the gospel see a poor person, they realize they are looking into a mirror. Their hearts must go out to him or her without an ounce of superiority or indifference.

In his letter to the church, James says that the poor Christian "ought to take pride in his high position" but the rich Christian "ought to take pride in his low position, because he will pass away like a wildflower" (James 1:9–10). This is a wonderfully paradoxical statement. Every Christian in Christ is at the same time a sinner who deserves death *and* also an adopted child of God, fully accepted and loved. This is true of Christians regardless of their social status. But James proposes that the well-off person who becomes a believer would spiritually benefit by especially thinking about her sinfulness before God, since out in the world she gets nothing but acclaim. On the other hand, the poor person who becomes a believer would spiritually benefit by especially thinking about her new high spiritual status, since out in the world she gets nothing but disdain.

Here we see why later James can say that concern for the poor and generous sharing of wealth are the inevitable signs of someone who has understood the gospel of grace. The world makes social class into bottom-line identities. You *are* your social status and bank account—that is the basis for your self-regard. But in the gospel these things are demoted and made peripheral. Someone who does not show any signs of at least gradual identity transformation in this manner does not give evidence of having really grasped the gospel. Thus James can say that faith without respect, love, and practical concern for the poor is dead. It's not justifying, gospel faith.

A New Attitude for the Poor

The gospel changes the identity of the well-off, so they have a new respect and love for the poor. But, as James says, the gospel also changes the self-understanding of the poor person. In an essay, "Shopkeeper's Gold," Croatian theologian Miroslav Volf tells of visiting Pastor Mark Gornik and walking the streets of Sandtown with him. The devastation of the U.S. neighborhood reminded Volf of Vukovar in his homeland, "but this time the destroyer was not war but racial tensions, crime, and economic ruin."[89] As they walked, Gornik made a point, "almost in passing," that startled Volf. As he was explaining the blight of the inner cities he suggested that the doctrine of justification by grace contains untapped resources for healing. "He should know," Volf thought. For some ten years he had been living and working in Sandtown and had seen transformation taking place, one house at a time.

Volf was shocked because, as a professor of theology at Yale, he knew that many in the church had completely abandoned the doctrine of justification. "They deem it generally useless or at least unhelpful when it comes to healing even lesser social pathologies than the cycle of poverty, violence, and hopelessness." Others retain their belief, and in fact fiercely defend it, but Volf had not heard any proponent of the classic teaching apply it as Gornik had. "How could the dead streets receive life from a [seemingly] dead doctrine?" he asked himself. But as he reflected, he got insight.

Imagine that you have no job, no money, you live cut off from the rest of society in a world ruled by poverty and violence, your skin is the "wrong" color—and you have no hope that any of this will change. Around you is a society governed by the iron law of achievement. Its gilded goods are flaunted before your eyes on TV screens, and in a thousand ways society tells you every day that you are worthless because you have no achievement. You are a failure, and you know that you will continue to be a failure because there is no way to achieve tomorrow what you have not managed to achieve today. Your dignity is shattered and your soul is enveloped in the darkness of despair. But the gospel tells you that you are not defined by outside forces. It tells you that you count; even more, that you are loved unconditionally and infinitely, irrespective of anything you have achieved or failed to achieve. Imagine now this gospel not simply proclaimed but embodied in a community. Justified by sheer grace, it seeks to "justify" by grace those declared "unjust" by a society's implacable law of achievement. Imagine, furthermore, this community determined to infuse the wider culture, along with its political and economic institutions, with the message that it seeks to embody and proclaim. This is justification by grace, proclaimed and practiced. A dead doctrine? Hardly![90]

Why Should We Do Justice?

"Pushing the Button"

Many people who are evidently genuine Christians do not demonstrate much concern for the poor. How do we account for that? I would like to believe that a heart for the poor "sleeps" down in a Christian's soul until it is awakened. I think the reason that this sensibility has not been more aroused in the Christian world is due to the failure of my own class—pastors and Christian leaders. We tend to try to develop a social conscience in Christians the same way the world does—through guilt. We tell them that they have so much and don't they see that they need to share with those who have so little. This doesn't work, because we have built-in defense mechanisms against such appeals. Almost no one really feels all that wealthy. Even the well-off don't feel rich compared to the others with whom they live and work.

I believe, however, when justice for the poor is connected not to guilt but to grace and to the gospel, this "pushes the button" down deep in believers' souls, and they begin to wake up. Here is an example of the kind of argument that accomplishes this. It comes from a sermon by a young Scottish minister early in the nineteenth century, preaching on the text "It is more blessed to give than to receive" (Acts 20:35):

Now, dear Christians, some of you pray night and day to be branches of the true Vine; you pray to be made all over in the image of Christ. If so, you must be like him in giving . . . "Though he was rich, yet for our sakes he became poor" . . . Objection 1. "My money is my own." Answer: Christ might have said, "My blood is my own, my life is my own" . . . then where should we have been? Objection 2. "The poor are undeserving." Answer: Christ might have said, "They are wicked rebels . . . shall I lay down my life for these? I will give to the good angels." But no, he left the ninety-nine, and came after the lost. He gave his blood for the undeserving. Objection 3. "The poor may abuse it." Answer: Christ might have said the same; yea, with far greater truth. Christ knew that thousands would trample his blood under their feet; that most would despise it; that many would make it an excuse for sinning more; yet he gave his own blood. Oh, my dear Christians! If you would be like Christ, give much, give often, give freely, to the vile and poor, the thankless and the undeserving. Christ is glorious and happy and so will you be. It is not your money I want, but your happiness. Remember his own word, "It is more blessed to give than to receive."[91]

SIX

HOW SHOULD WE DO JUSTICE?

If I have denied the desires of the poor or let the eyes of the widow grow weary, if I have kept my bread to myself, not sharing it . . . if I have raised my hand against the fatherless, knowing that I had influence in court, then let my arm fall from the shoulder, let it be broken off at the joint.

Job 31:16–19

Doing justice is an important part of living the Christian life in the world. I personally came to that conclusion long ago. What I have wrestled with for many years since is the question of *how* to practically answer this call today.

Always Thinking of Justice

When Job says, "I put on righteousness as my clothing; justice was my robe and turban" (Job 29:14), he is speaking about a social consciousness that infused his daily life as completely as his clothing covered his body.[92] He shared his money and food with the poor. He cared for the blind, the crippled, and the poor widow. He was also a legal advocate for the immigrant and the orphan.

The vision is comprehensive. Job says he *wears* justice, suggesting that it is always on his mind, he is always looking for ways to do it. Psalm 41:1 says, "Blessed is the man who considers the poor," and the Hebrew word translated as "considers" means to give sustained attention to a subject and then to act wisely and successfully with regard to it. God does not want us to merely give the poor perfunctory help, but to ponder long and hard about how to improve their entire situation.[93]

A Christian man I know owns a chain of car dealerships. As is standard practice in the industry, his salesmen were authorized to negotiate the price of the car with their customers. At one point, however, the CEO did some research and uncovered the fact that, in general, men were more persistent negotiators than women, and Anglos pressed their interests much more determinedly than African-Americans. In other words, black women, who were often poorer, were paying more for cars than more prosperous customers. The owner realized that this time-honored business practice took advantage of a class of people that needed help and protection. The policy was obviously not illegal, and few people would have considered it immoral. But it ended up being exploitative. So the company changed the policy to one of no negotiation—the listed price was *the* price. This would not have occurred to most people, but this Christian businessman was "considering" the poor, and seeking to integrate the doing of justice into all aspects of his private and public life.

I once asked him, was this "good business" on his part? He replied that that there may be some future benefits for the company but that they would be minor, unquantifiable, and they didn't matter. They made the changes because the practice was taking economic advantage of people with fewer resources. "Do not take advantage of a widow," said Exodus 22:22. Most ethics courses in business school provide many case studies in which business owners and employees are urged to do the honest and just thing. But what motivation is given? Here is a typical answer:

> Businesses can often attain short-term gains by acting in an unethical fashion; however, such behaviors tend to undermine the economy over time.[94]

The argument is: Be ethical, and you will gain a long-term advantage for yourself and your business.

But the Bible says that the righteous disadvantage themselves to advantage others, while "the wicked . . . are willing to disadvantage the community to advantage themselves."[95] In this case, the Christian business owner was willing to permanently disadvantage his business, if it meant doing justice.

Doing justice, then, requires constant, sustained reflection and circumspection. If you are a Christian, and you refrain from committing adultery or using profanity or missing church, but you don't do the hard work of thinking through how to do justice in every area of life—you are failing to live justly and righteously.[96]

Levels of Help

Often we don't need to go looking for opportunities to do justice. Churches and Christians who seek to do justice have poor families and neighborhoods nearby. The problems seem vast and intractable. How do we even begin to think about how we can help?

Mary was a woman whose husband was descending into a downward spiral of addiction and anger. The family's debts grew to insupportable levels. She had been out of the workforce for many years to raise her children and had no marketable skills, no individual credit record, and no savings. Other members of her family lived at some distance and in any case had no financial resources to offer her. Her husband was at first opposed to her going back to work, and later he left the family.

Mary approached the diaconate of our Redeemer Church in New York City with much fear and trepidation. In many ways she was in the same position as the widows of ancient times—socially and economically vulnerable, without the social capital with which to bring her family through the difficulties. The deacons and deaconesses helped Mary at first by giving her money from the church's diaconal fund for basic household expenses, and then by walking with her through the long process of achieving financial self-sufficiency, including finding a job, learning to deal with lawyers and judges, and getting a more affordable apartment. Just as crucial as all other forms of help, Mary got love and new friendship as well as professional counseling, which helped her through her time of personal crisis.[97]

Mary illustrates the fact that vulnerable people need multiple levels of help. We will call these layers *relief, development,* and *social reform.* Relief is direct aid to meet immediate physical, material, and economic needs. The Good Samaritan provided relief when he gave physical protection, emergency medical treatment, and a rent subsidy (Luke 10:30–35). Common relief ministries are temporary shelters for the homeless and refugees, food and clothing services for people in need, and free or low-cost medical and counseling services. Relief also means caring for foster children, the elderly, and the physically handicapped through home care or the establishment of institutions. A more assertive form of relief is advocacy, in which people in need are given active assistance to find legal aid, housing, and other kinds of help, such as protection from various forms of domestic abuse and violence.

The next level is *development*. This means giving an individual, family, or entire community what they need to move beyond dependency on relief into a condition of economic self-sufficiency. In the Old Testament, when a slave's debt was erased and he was released, God directed that his former master send him out with sufficient grain, tools, and resources for a new, self-sufficient economic life (Deuteronomy 15:13–14). Old Testament scholar Christopher Wright urges us to think out the implications of the various Old Testament laws of release, gleaning, and Jubilee for our own time. Wright says:

[God's] law asks us . . . to find means of ensuring that the weakest and poorest in the community are enabled to have access to the opportunities they need in order to provide for themselves.

[*114*]

"Opportunities" may include financial resources, but could also include access to education, legal assistance, investment in job opportunities, etc. Such things should not be leftovers or handouts, but a matter of rights. . . .[98]

Wright then lays out a good list of what is entailed in helping a poor family or individual climb out of a state of constant dependency. It includes education, job creation and training, job search skills, and financial counseling as well as helping a family into home ownership. "Development," of course, is far more time consuming, complex, and expensive than relief.

The Needs of Poor Communities

We have considered what it takes to help an individual or a family. But what does it take to help entire neighborhoods to self-sufficiency? Most of the best answers to that question begin with a look at the life and work of John M. Perkins. Perkins, born in 1930, founded ministries in both rural and urban areas of Mississippi, as well as urban Los Angeles. His work has included a dizzying variety of programs, including day care, farm co-ops, health centers, adult education centers, low-income housing development, tutoring, job training, youth internships, and college scholarship programs, as well as very vigorous evangelism and new church planting.[99] Perkins's approach at the time was revolutionary, because he combined very traditional, evangelical Christian theology and ministry with a holistic vision for both ministry to the whole person and rebuilding entire poor communities.

Charles Marsh, professor at the University of Virginia, makes a strong case that Perkins and his movement have taken up and carried on Martin Luther King, Jr.'s vision for "the beloved community."[100] After King's death, Marsh argues, the Civil Rights Movement lost its "unifying spiritual vision"—its belief that social reform could come through grassroots, local communities of faith. The movement came to rely completely on politics and government. But without denying the importance of public policies such as integration, equal employment opportunity, and welfare, "Perkins . . . concluded that government programs alone failed to address the deeper sources of hopelessness in black communities."[101]

When Perkins tied social reform, economic development, and vigorous evangelism all together into a seamless whole, he confounded both the secularized liberal civil rights establishment and the conservative churches. Leaders of both sides did not know how to regard him, but many younger Christian leaders were inspired, and in 1989 they formed the Christian

Community Development Association, which now includes hundreds of churches and local development corporations.

Relocation and Redistribution

When John Perkins explained his philosophy of ministry, he always named three basic factors. One he called "relocation," though others have called it "reneighboring a community." Traditional private charity and most government programs provide help to the poor, but service providers do not live in the community and therefore have no firsthand knowledge of the needs of the neighborhood, or any real accountability to the residents.[102] Perkins advocated that those helping the neighborhood live in it.

Perkins also spoke of "redistribution," something others have called "reweaving a community." John Perkins saw that simply putting welfare checks in the hands of the poor in small towns only ended up transferring capital into the accounts of the wealthy bankers and store owners on the other side of town. A healthy neighborhood is one with safe streets, responsive public institutions, physical beauty, good schools, a good economy, good social-recreational opportunities, and wide participation in political life.[103] "Reweaving" aims to bring these things about. There must be a full range of measures designed to redirect the flow of financial capital, social capital, and spiritual capital back into the community instead of out of it.

By "financial capital," we of course mean the ability to attract businesses that not only provide goods for customers, but also keep wealth and financial capital in the community itself. Typically, in blighted neighborhoods there are few jobs, and the businesses that are there (even the banks) are those that take capital from local consumers to spend and invest it in other neighborhoods.[104] Even the employers that do exist in poor communities—such as hospitals, clinics, government centers, and schools—usually employ people who neither live nor spend their income in the neighborhood where they work. All this creates a flow of financial capital out of the community.

By "social capital," Perkins meant the training and retaining of local leadership. For this to occur, the local schools must be strong and local businesses and institutions must employ people from the community, since that is the way that persons become more valuable and productive as they grow in their skills. Typically, in blighted neighborhoods, the schools are failing and the businesses and institutions are run by people who do not live there. All this creates a flow of "social capital" out of the community.

"Spiritual capital" refers to the spiritual and moral

influence of the churches in the neighborhood. The weakening of neighborhoods economically and socially goes hand-in-hand with their spiritual weakening. Strong Christians and churches have left as fast as, if not faster than, others.

Mark Gornik makes it clear that if we are talking of community development, it must mean that the people of the community are "the primary agents of action." The community residents themselves must be the main "locus of analysis and planning" and they must be in control of the type and pace of change that will affect their families, lives, and economic life.[105] Any other kind of "help" usually keeps residents in dependency, because it doesn't really bring social and economic capital into the neighborhood. Business owners and agency heads need to be neighbors, living their lives there, spending their money there, bringing their real estate values and relational networks there. That is what rebuilds community.

Racial Reconciliation

There is a third important factor in John Perkins's strategy for rebuilding poor communities. He names it "racial reconciliation." In both private charity and government agencies, many of the providers are of a different race than the care receivers. While Perkins insisted that leadership for development be based in poor communities, he also "invited outsiders [usually Anglo] to play a critical role in fostering indigenous leadership." He did this while many civil rights organizations "often radicalized and politicized the role of the outsider at the expense of people in poor communities."[106]

These two factors—inviting outsiders to play a role along with insisting that the residents of poor communities be empowered to control their own destiny— meant that the leadership for community development had to be multiethnic and interracial. It is always much easier for the leaders to be of one race—whether just indigenous members of the community or only professional helpers from outside the neighborhood. But Perkins knew that the combination, if it could be made to work, was powerful. This was one of Perkins's most important contributions and challenges. What is best for the poor community—a nonpaternalistic partnership of people from different races and social locations— was also one of the gifts that the gospel makes possible.

The Bible provides deep resources for racial rapprochement. Its depiction of creation cuts the nerve of racism at its source. It insists that all human beings are "of one blood" (Acts 17:26). The account of Adam's creation is crucial for an understanding of race. Here is a comment from the *Mishnah*, the first major commentary on the Bible compiled by Jewish Bible scholars. "Why did God create only one human being? So that no one can say to a fellow human being: My father was better than yours."[107] Because all are created in the image of God, no one race is inherently superior to any other.

Where does racism come from? In Genesis 11, the story of the Tower of Babel tells us that the people of the earth were marked by pride and a lust for power. As due punishment for this pride, we are told that God "confused their speech." They could not understand each other or work together and as a result they scattered into different nations. We must not miss the profound message of this account—that human pride and lust for power leads to racial and national division, strife, and hatred. One scholar sums up the teaching of the passage like this: "The division into different people groups with different languages was a consequence of human disobedience."[108] Immediately thereafter, in Genesis 12, God comes to Abraham and promises to bring a salvation into the world that will bless "all the families [*mispahah*] of the earth." This word "families" means people-groups, nations, or races. God is distressed that the unity of the human family has been broken, and declares his intention to take down the walls of racism and nationalism that human sin and pride have put there.

Grace and Race

The New Testament completes the story. In Acts 2, when the Holy Spirit descends on the church on the day of Pentecost, another miracle occurs. While at Babel people who spoke the same language couldn't understand each other, at Pentecost, everyone who spoke different languages could nonetheless all understand the preaching of the gospel by the apostles. It was a reversing of the curse of Babel. It was a declaration that the grace of Jesus can heal the wounds of racism. At Pentecost the first gospel preaching was in every language, showing that no one culture is *the* "right" culture, and that in the Spirit we can have a unity that transcends all national, linguistic, and cultural barriers. The result, according to Ephesians 2:11–22, is a community of equal "fellow-citizens" from all races. According to 1 Peter 2:9, Christians are a "new ethnic." Partnership and friendship across racial barriers within the church is one of the signs of the presence and power of the gospel. In Christ our racial and cultural identities, while not insignificant, are no longer primary to our self-understanding. Our bond with others in Christ is stronger than our relationship to other members of our own racial and national groups. The gospel makes us all like Abraham, who left his home culture but never "arrived" in another one. So, for example, Chinese Christians do not renounce their Chinese identity to become something else, yet the gospel gives them critical distance from their own culture, enabling them to critique their own cultural idols.

In the final chapters of the Bible, a time is envisioned in which God's people are united from "every tribe and language and people and nation" (Revelations 5:9; 7:9; 11:9; 14:6). At the climax of the world's history, brought about by the death and resurrection of Jesus, there will be the end of all racial division and hatred.

Between the promise of Genesis 12 and its fulfillment in Revelation, the Bible strikes numerous blows against racism. Moses's sister Miriam was punished by God because she rejected Moses's African wife on account of her race (Numbers 12). Jonah was condemned because he regarded Nineveh primarily on the basis of race and politics (their prosperity threatened Israel), instead of on the basis of their spiritual need. The apostle Peter, through a vision and the conversion of Cornelius the Gentile centurion, was taught about the sinfulness of racial and ethnic bias (Acts 9:34).[109] He was brought to see that "God does not show favoritism but accepts *from every nation* those who fear him and do what is right" (Acts 9:35–37). Despite this testimony, sometime later the apostle Paul saw Peter refusing to eat with Gentile Christians, and he confronted him about his racism. He told Peter he was "not acting *in line with the gospel*" (Galatians 2:14). To act "in line with the gospel" is to live consistently with the truth that we are sinners saved by sheer grace. Racial prejudice is wrong because it is a denial of the very principle that all human beings are equally sinful and saved by only the grace of God. A deep grasp of the gospel of grace, Paul says, should erode our racial biases. One Christian theologian wrote:

> Once faith is exercised, a Christian is free . . . to wear his culture like a comfortable suit of clothes. He can shift to other cultural clothing temporarily if he wishes to do so, as Paul suggests in I Corinthians 9:19–23, and he is released to admire and appreciate the differing expressions of Christ shining out through other cultures.[110]

The Bible's theological attack on racism is powerful, and in response many idealistic Christians have set out to form communities that are "multicultural," but this is far, far easier said than done. There is no such thing as a neutral, culture-free way to do anything. If you form a governing board made up of people from different races, how will your board go about making decisions? Anglo, African-American, Hispanic, and Asian cultures all have distinct approaches to things like fact-finding, authority, persuasion, time frames, ratification of agreements, and so on. So which culture's way of decision-making will prevail? And why should it be *that* culture's method? I fear that attempting to craft a culture-free way to make decisions as a group is somewhat naïve.

Despite the cultural differences, the Bible says that these barriers can and must be overcome. What Christians have in common goes deeper than their cultural dissimilarities. And because the gospel gives Christians a new critical distance from their own race's perspective and values, they have the ability to reach out and better work with people of other cultures, whether they believe the Christian faith or not. When this theology of grace and race permeates the consciousness of a Christian, a church, and a community, the resulting unity of relationships becomes both a means to re-neighboring and reweaving and a direct witness to the world of the reality of the gospel.[111]

Reform and Changing Systems

We said that there were three "levels" for doing justice and helping the needy. Besides relief and development (both individual and corporate) there is social reform. Social reform moves beyond the relief of immediate needs and dependency and seeks to change the conditions and social structures that aggravate or cause that dependency. Imagine a sequel to the Good Samaritan parable. The months go by and every time he makes his trip from Jerusalem to Jericho he finds another man in the road, beaten and robbed. Finally the Samaritan says, "How do we stop the violence?"

The answer to that question would be some kind of social reform—instituting a new social arrangement that stops the flow of victims because of a change in social conditions. Sometimes the social reform that works is simply putting more police on the street. But another way to accomplish the goal would be an effort like the TenPoint Coalition, a network of Boston clergy who sought to stem the tide of gang killings in Boston in the 1990s. The coalition built bridges between institutions that previously had not worked together or that had even worked against one another. It partnered with families, local churches, and the Boston Police Department and U.S. District Attorney's Office to do gang mediation and intervention, and reentry mentoring for ex-offenders, and to provide other services.[112] This approach goes beyond just helping individuals. It seeks to change social arrangements and social institutions. In some cases, it means changing laws.

How Should We Do Justice?

We have discussed how careful we must be in applying the Mosaic social legislation to our present society. Yet the Bible gives us examples of people who were zealous for social justice outside of the nation-state of Israel. As we have seen, Job is a prime example.[113] He tells us that he not only clothed the naked, but he "broke the fangs of the wicked and made them drop their victims" (Job 29:17). Daniel called a pagan government to account for its lack of mercy to the poor (Daniel 4:27). These are examples of what we have been calling "rectifying" justice. Everywhere we look we see the need for this kind of justice. There are city agencies that are not fair in the attention and resources they give to middle-class and wealthy neighborhoods over poor ones. There are judges who take bribes, legislators who are "bought" by special interest money, banking policies that discriminate against neighborhoods, building code inspectors in the pocket of landlords and real estate interests, and corruption within the law enforcement system. To address and rectify these practices is to do social reform.

Many Christians resist the idea that social systems need to be dealt with directly. They prefer the idea that "society is changed one heart at a time," and so they concentrate on only evangelism and individual social work. This is naïve. One of the most poignant examples of this naïveté I know is a story told by an urban pastor, Robert Linthicum.

As a student ministry intern he had been working among black teenagers in a government housing project in a U.S. city. A fourteen-year-old girl named Eva began to attend one of the Bible studies that he led in the project. At one point Eva came to him, deeply troubled. "Bob," she said, "I am under terrible pressure and I don't know what to do. There is a very large gang in this project that recruits girls to be prostitutes for wealthy white men in the suburbs. They are trying to force me . . ." He urged her not to give in to their demands and to stick with her Bible study group. He then went home for his summer vacation.

"Three months later I returned and Eva was nowhere to be found. The other youth told me she had stopped coming about a month after I had left. I went to Eva's apartment. As soon as she saw me she burst into tears. 'They got to me, Bob,' she said. 'How could you give in like that?' I unsympathetically responded. 'Why didn't you resist?' She told me a story of terror. 'First they told me they would beat my father . . . and they beat him bad. I had no alternative. So I gave in.' 'But, Eva,' I said, 'why didn't you get some protection? Why didn't you go to the police?' Eva responded, 'Who do you think *they* are?'"[114]

How Should We Do Justice?

Linthicum goes on to say that until that moment he had thought of sin in strictly individualistic terms. He began to realize that much of the city's legal and political system was arrayed to enrich and empower people at the expense of the poor. There was no way to rescue the "Evas" of the city without waiting on those systems.

As terrible as Linthicum's story is, oppression and injustice take even more virulent forms in many parts of the world. The list includes abusive child labor and sex-trafficking, state-sponsored religious persecution, detention without trial or charges, seizure of private land without due process and payment, forced migration, organized violence against ethnic minorities, state, rebel, or paramilitary terrorism, and state-sponsored torture.[116]

One problem with the illustrations I've given is that they are so stark and obvious. Most of the time systemic evil is simpler and more subtle. Failing schools and inadequate police protection in poor neighborhoods are far more common. It is often the result of unjust neglect. Our political and economic systems do not listen to people without money and other forms of social power. The residents of poor communities do not have either the influence or the skills to attract more private and public resources to come into their community. They need help, but it can't come merely in the form of relief and development. Someone must resist and change the legal, political, and social systems.

Putting It All Together

Doing justice in poor communities includes direct relief, individual development, community development, racial reconciliation, and social reform.

One of the best examples I know that combines all these aspects of "doing justice" is the work of New Song Church in the Sandtown area of Baltimore, Maryland, which I have referred to several times in this volume. When Mark Gornik, his friends Allan and Susan Tibbels, and the Tibbels' two young daughters moved into the very poor African-American inner-city community, LaVerne Stokes, a lifelong resident of Sandtown, wrote,

> It was the first time we had ever seen white people move in. I wondered what it was they wanted. They rehabbed vacant houses and moved into them, hung out on the streets and attended community meetings, and spent time with the children of Sandtown, including my children. . . .

[W]hen Pastor Mark and the Tibbels began a church together with families from the neighborhood, my kids asked me to go visit, which I did. . . . [They] showed a deep love for the community, *my* community, and became my neighbors. Together we began ministries to love our community and rebuild it, restore it to the health and vibrancy I had experienced as a little girl. This effort included creating programs in housing, education, and health care, as well as programs in job development, economic development, and development of the arts.[117]

Alongside the church was a church-based community development corporation known as New Song Urban Ministries, which today employs a staff of over eighty people, working in the Sandtown-Winchester area of West Baltimore. They concentrate mainly on a fifteen-block area in the north-central part of the neighborhood. The ministries include Sandtown Habitat for Humanity, which has completed two hundred homes since the mid-1980s, Eden Jobs, which has placed over a thousand people in jobs, with plans for one hundred annually, a family health center, a Community Learning Center including preschool, after-school programs, a scholarship program, and New Song Academy, which is a K-8 public school under the New Schools Initiative. Gornik lays out an overarching scheme that shows how all of these aspects of justice can be brought together. He names three basic roles that churches can play in poor communities.

Churches in poor neighborhoods can serve as *healing communities*. He quotes a text that puts this in social-science terms. He says congregations: "offer . . . narratives that help individuals navigate economic difficulties, sickness, and domestic trouble."[118] Put better, "For young people faced with the dangers of the street, the church is a place of literal salvation; for women faced with added burdens of oppression, the church is a shelter from the storm; for people in recovery, the church is a support system." It is a place of healing and grace.

Christians can form organizations that serve as *healers of communities*. By this Gornik means what we have called "development." He includes "operating credit unions and neighborhood banks; creating, retaining, and attracting jobs; developing and managing houses for families and the elderly; educating children in after-school programs and religiously based schools; and providing preventative and primary health care for the uninsured and underserved."

Finally, churches encourage people to be *organizers for just communities*. These are ways that the church can challenge and change social systems. This includes especially mobilizing people to create local "schools that educate children" and "public services that maintain communities."[119]

What about the Rest of Us?

There are hundreds of urban churches that are using Perkins's model of Christian community development, and literally tens of thousands of inner city churches that are carrying out a dizzying variety of "holistic" ministries. But many will ask, "But what about the rest of us? Most Christians don't live—and most churches aren't located—in communities of poverty." Even if we grant that more Christians should live with the poor and more churches should be planted there, that doesn't answer the question. What should you do if you and your church are not in located in areas of poverty or dire need?

You or your church should begin by discovering the needs in your locale. Are there disadvantaged children (abused and neglected, physically or mentally disabled, failing in school) who could use help? Are there elderly, disabled, single parents, chronically ill, or new immigrants who need aid? Are there poor families around that are invisible to you? To learn about these needs, Christians and churches need to do much more sustained listening to their community's leaders than they are used to doing.

When Redeemer Church purchased property in a neighborhood in Manhattan, we visited both with the neighborhood's city councilwoman and the local community board. Our questions were: What are the needs here that you and the community feel are both chronic and acute? What could we do that would make this neighborhood a better place to live in? Even though, as of this writing, we are only beginning to hear the answers to these questions, we were gratified at the response. Everyone we have approached has been surprised that a church would even ask. Ordinarily, churches and other religious institutions assume they know best what the community needs.

Another thing that your church can do is to make a connection to churches and ministries that are resident and effective in poorer neighborhoods and poorer countries. Ask them what they need from you, and likely the answer will be requests for volunteers, pro bono work from professionals, funding, and perhaps even some of your church's best leaders coming and living and working with them in the communities of need.[120] But let *them* tell *you*.

Working with People in Need

Many believe that the job of the church is not to do justice at all, but to preach the Word, to evangelize and build up believers. But if it is true that justice and mercy to the poor are the inevitable signs of justifying faith, it is hard to believe that the church is not to reflect this duty corporately in some way. And as soon as you get involved in the lives of people—in evangelism as well as spiritual nurture—you will come upon people with practical needs. You can't love people in word only (cf. 1 John 3:16–17) and therefore you can't love people as you are doing evangelism and discipleship without meeting practical and material needs through deeds.

As we have seen, a special class of officers—deacons—was established to coordinate the church's ministry of sharing money and goods with those in need within the community. 2 Corinthians 8:13–14 and Galatians 2:10 show actual case studies of corporate *diakonia,* in which the church gave offerings and relief to the poor, those offerings being administered by leaders appointed by the church.

As soon as a church engages in holistic ministry, however, it will run up against a number of practical policy issues. Often people with the same basic vision for justice will disagree on the specific answers to the following questions. Any church or group of Christians who want to make progress in this work will have to take the time to come to a consensus on how to answer each one.

How much should we help? Any church or group of Christians who are serving people with material needs will find that the ministry is expensive. Many will ask just how much of a priority should a church give it in relationship to other ministries. Should a church wait until it is big and established before it begins to reach out to the community? The needs seem to be endless. What percentage of the church's energy and money should go into it?

Whom should we help? Should you help only people who seek you out? Or should you deliberately approach a particular class of people in need? And how "needy" must someone be before the church helps him or her? In chapter 4 we looked at Jonathan Edwards's wise counsel about this issue. He argues that we should not wait until a person is destitute. Nevertheless, it is difficult to know "where to draw the line." Churches and Christian organizations must not be wooden and mechanical, yet they will have to come up with

some agreed-upon guidelines, or find themselves
endlessly arguing.

*Under what conditions does your help proceed or
end?* Do you require that the persons you help
attend your church? Should there be other qual-
ifications? Should your aid give priority to church
members but also extend to others, as Galatians
6:10 and other Biblical texts seem to indicate?
Some point to the standards for widows that
the church supported in 1 Timothy 5:1–10, and
argue that these should be strict requirements
for giving aid.[121] But in Acts 4 we saw that the
Christians shared their possessions in such a way
that every needy believer had his or her needs
met from the common funds of the church (Acts
4:34).

In what way do we help? We mentioned that
deed ministry can consist of three levels—relief,
development, and reform. Will your church be
sticking to relief type efforts only, or will it try
ministries within the more ambitious and complex levels? Will your church work almost exclusively with needy individuals and their families,
or will it seek to reach out to particular needy
classes of people, such as the homebound elderly,

or youth who need tutoring, or prisoners and ex-offenders?

From where should we help? Should people from your church move into areas of need or work from where they already live in partnership with churches, institutions, and organizations in the neighborhood? Will "moving in" only lead to gentrification?

As your group of believers works through these questions, always try to err on the side of being generous, and always keep your policies flexible and open to cases that don't fit your categories.

Doing Justice and Preaching Grace

As Christians do justice, they must face the important practical issue of how justice relates to their other duties as believers. In particular, what is the relationship between the call to help the needy and the Biblical command to evangelize?

Some have argued that Christians should only do justice as a means to the end of evangelism. That is, we should do mercy and justice only because it helps us bring people to faith in Christ.[122] This does not seem to fit in with Jesus's Good Samaritan parable and his charge not to give to needy people in order to get something in return (Luke 6:32–35). Though Jesus has in view people who can repay us financially, the basic principle is that we are not to give expecting gratitude (verse 32). If we only help people who are responding to the gospel, we will be perceived as only helping others in order to help ourselves, namely, to increase our own numbers.

On the other hand, there are many who insist that doing justice *is* spreading the gospel, it *is* evangelism they say. Doing justice can indeed lead people to give the message of gospel grace a hearing, but to consider deeds of mercy and justice to be identical to gospel proclamation is a fatal confusion. I propose a different way to understand evangelism and social justice. They should exist in an asymmetrical, inseparable relationship.

Evangelism is the most basic and radical ministry possible to a human being. This is true not because the spiritual is more important than the physical, but because the eternal is more important than the temporal. In 2 Corinthians 4:16–18 Paul speaks of the importance of strengthening the "inner man" even as the outer, physical nature is aging and decaying. If there is a God, and if life with him for eternity is based on having a saving relationship with him, then the most loving thing anyone can do for one's neighbor is help him or her to a saving faith in that God.

But, as we have seen, doing justice is inseparably connected to preaching grace. This is true in two ways. One way is that the gospel produces a concern for the poor. The other is that deeds of justice gain credibility for the preaching of the gospel. In other words, justification by faith leads to doing justice, and doing justice can make many seek to be justified by faith.

In the book of Acts we see this dynamic illustrated. In Acts 2 the descent of the Holy Spirit and the disciples' encounter with God led to radical sharing with the needy (verse 44–45). There was no reason that the church "grew in favor with all the people" (verse 47). The experience of salvation led to generosity to the poor, which led to more people becoming open to the message of salvation. In Acts 4 we read, similarly, that the economic sharing of the people inside the church lent great power to the preaching of the resurrection to those outside the church (Acts 4:32–35). Finally, in Acts 6, after the ministry of *diakonia* is more firmly established, Luke adds: "So the word of God spread. The number of disciples in Jerusalem increased rapidly" (verse 7). The word "so" indicates a cause-effect relationship. This sharing of resources across class lines—between the "needy" and those wealthy enough to have property to sell— was extremely rare in the Greco-Roman world. The practical actions of Christians for people in need was therefore striking to observers and made them open to the gospel message. The Roman emperor Julian despised the Christian faith, but he candidly admitted that Christianity was constantly gaining new converts because believers' generosity to the poor made it so attractive.

> Nothing has contributed to the progress of the superstition of the Christians as their charity to strangers . . . the impious Galileans provide not only for their own poor, but for ours as well.[123]

I urge my readers to discern the balance I am seeking to strike. If we confuse evangelism and social justice we lose what is the single most unique service that Christians can offer the world. Others, alongside believers, can feed the hungry. But Christians have the gospel of Jesus by which men and women can be born again into the certain hope of eternal life. No one else can make such an invitation. However, many Christians who care intensely about evangelism see the work of doing justice as a distraction for Christians that detracts from the mission of evangelism. That is also a grave error.

Imagine an eloquent Christian preacher who every Sunday delivers compelling sermons. But one of his female parishioners comes to learn that the minister verbally abuses and browbeats his wife daily. After she discovers this, she unsurprisingly finds his sermons completely unpersuasive. Why? His deeds contradict his words, and so his words have no power. Imagine instead a new minister whose public oratory is quite mediocre. However, as time goes on, the parishioners come to see that he is a man of sterling character, wisdom, humility, and love. Soon, because of the quality of his life, his members will find that they are hanging on every word of his preaching.

When a city perceives a church as existing strictly and only for itself and its own members, the preaching of that church will not resonate with outsiders. But if neighbors see church members loving their city through astonishing, sacrificial deeds of compassion, they will be much more open to the church's message. Deeds of mercy and justice should be done out of love, not simply as a means to the end of evangelism. And yet there is no better way for Christians to lay a foundation for evangelism than by doing justice.[124]

It is also impossible to separate word and deed ministry from each other in ministry because human beings are integrated wholes—body and soul. When some Christians say, "Caring for physical needs will detract from evangelism," they must be thinking only of doing evangelism among people who are comfortable and well-off. The London City Mission is a nearly two-hundred-year-old evangelical mission that seeks to do evangelism among the urban poor of London. Though evangelism is its central purpose, this is done through relationship, visitation, and friendship. Its mission is: *the same person, going to the same people, regularly, to become their friend for Jesus's sake.* Because of this mission, LCM missionaries run neither large-scale evangelism nor social programs. Instead "word" and "deed" are seamlessly integrated in their ministry. Helping their neighbors with their children's educational needs, or with finding jobs or learning English as a second language, goes hand-in-hand with sharing their faith verbally. On paper, we may ask, "Should Christians do evangelism or social justice?" But in real life, these things go together.[125]

Christians who live or work in needy communities in order to do evangelism must inevitably become involved in helping their friends and neighbors with their pressing economic and social needs. To fail to do so is simply a lack of love. It is also impractical. If you wish to share your faith with needy people, and you do nothing about the painful conditions in which they live, you will fail to show them Christ's beauty. We must neither confuse evangelism with doing justice, nor separate them from one another.

Spheres of Justice

There is one more practical issue that believers must face when considering how to do justice. Should believers act as individuals out in the world or through their local church? What exactly is the role of the local church in the work of justice?

The church should help believers shape every area of their lives with the gospel. When Jonathan Edwards was teaching his people about how to live their lives, he continually referred to "the rules of the gospel." By that he meant the logic of God's salvation in Jesus. He reasoned, "If you are a sinner saved by grace, how should that influence your civic life? Your attitude toward the poor?" All churches should do the same with their members.

But that doesn't mean that the church as an institution is itself to do everything it equips its members to do. For example, while the church should disciple its members who are filmmakers so that their cinematic art will be profoundly influenced by the gospel, that does not mean that the church should establish a company that produces feature films. No institution or organization can do all things well—that goes for the Christian church as well.

At this point the concept of Abraham Kuyper's "sphere sovereignty" can be of some help. Kuyper was both a Christian minister and the prime minister of the Netherlands at the turn of the twentieth century. As both a theologian and a politician, he was able to reflect on the respective roles of church, state, and voluntary associations. Kuyper concluded that the institutional church's mission is to evangelize and nurture believers in Christian community. As it does this work, it produces people who engage in art, science, education, journalism, filmmaking, business, in distinctive ways as believers in Christ. The church, in this view, produces individuals who change society, but the local congregation should not itself engage in these enterprises. Kuyper distinguished between the institutional church—the congregation meeting under its leaders—and the "organic" church, which consists of all Christians, functioning in the world as individuals and through various agencies and voluntary organizations. [126]

I believe Kuyper is generally right. We have spoken of different "levels" of ministry to the poor—relief, development, and reform. As we have said, churches under their leaders should definitely carry out ministries of relief and some development among their own members and in their neighborhoods and cities, as the natural and crucial way to show the world God's character, and to love the people that they are evangelizing and discipling. But if we apply Kuyper's view, then when we get to the more ambitious work of social reform and the addressing of social structure, believers should work through associations and organizations rather than through the local church. While the institutional church should do relief inside and around its community, the "organic" church should be doing development and social reform. [127]

This is not just a theological principle, it is also a very practical issue. Many of the churches who practice John Perkins's model of ministry form community development corporations, distinct from their congregations, to operate programs in the community. This frees the pastors and leaders of the local church to build up the church through evangelism and discipleship, and it enables laypeople who are skilled in other fields to provide leadership over the various ministries that major in doing justice. Churches that, against Kuyper's advice, try to take on all the levels of doing justice often find that the work of community renewal and social justice overwhelms the work of preaching, teaching, and nurturing the congregation.[128]

Doing justice necessitates striking a series of balances. It means ministering in both word and deed, through the local church and as individual agents dispersed throughout the world. It means engaging in relief, and development, and reform. We do all this not only because we learn from the Bible that the causes of poverty are complex, but also because the gospel of Christ gives us such an arsenal of different weapons against the forces of injustice and deprivation in the world. But none of the weapons is a literal weapon. That is not the kind of warfare we wage. As the well-known hymn says, "'Tis not with swords loud clashing, nor roll of stirring drums, but deeds of love and mercy, the heav'nly kingdom comes."

CHAPTER 7
❀❀❀

DOING JUSTICE
IN THE PUBLIC SQUARE

*Seek justice, encourage the oppressed. Defend the
cause of the fatherless, plead the case of the widow.*

Isaiah 1:17

When Christians do evangelism, they can only
count on the support and understanding of
other believers. But when believers seek to do justice in
the world, they often find it both necessary and desir-
able to work with others who do not share their faith.
Christians who are concerned to do justice in particular
neighborhoods—or who want to work for some social
reform such as the betterment of public schools, or the
end of ethnic "cleansing" in another part of the world,
or the elimination of "sweatshops" in urban areas—will
find many allies who are willing to work with them.[129]

Should Christians work together for justice in society with members of other religions or no religion?

If so, how should they do it? In order to answer these questions, we must first take a look at the public square in late modern society, where discussions about the definition of justice have almost completely broken down.

"This Is a Justice Issue"

I once heard a debate among several staff members of a nonprofit organization over who should get the privilege of representing the agency at an important conference. Some believed that it should be the female member of the staff who had the most seniority. Others proposed a younger man who, though having served for fewer years, was unusually gifted in public presentation. Those backing the woman grew more and more agitated during the conversation. Finally, one said, "I'm sorry, but for me this is a *justice* issue." There was an abrupt, awkward silence. Soon the group agreed to award the conference trip to the woman, but it was clear that the backers of the young man felt they had been steamrollered. Why? It was because in our society naming something a "justice issue" is a kind of trump card. If you are arguing against someone who suddenly proclaims that his position is the one that promotes justice, there is no defense. To continue to press your argument is to stand on the side of injustice, and who wants to do that?

There's a big problem with this move, however. Those staff members who were backing the young man were not convinced. They valued ability over seniority, but instead of discussing these two sets of values on their merits, one group simply labeled the other group's position unjust. The woman's supporters had won the battle but had created resentment.

The reason it is not convincing to simply cry "injustice!" is that our society is deeply divided over the very definition of justice. Nearly everyone thinks they are on justice's side. Both pro-life and pro-choice partisans frame their position as the one that is on the side of justice. Both opponents and proponents of affirmative action insist that their way is the way of equity and the other side is perpetrating unfairness. But underneath all the name calling are sharp differences of opinion about what justice actually is. Democrats think of it more in collective terms. They believe a low tax rate is unfair because it deprives the poor and minorities of the help they need to overcome years of discrimination. Republicans think of justice more individualistically. They believe that a high tax rate is unjust because it robs people of their due who have risked much and worked hard to keep what they earn.

The fact is that the word "justice" does not have a definition in our culture that we can all agree on. So we just use it as a bludgeon. We self-righteously imply that those on the other side *know* they are simply being unjust. But they don't.

Empty Concepts

"Wait," you may say. "Isn't justice a matter of common sense? Isn't it simply respect for equality and individual freedom?" But these terms "freedom" and "equality," as they are used in our society today, do not help us much in defining justice.

Michael J. Klarman of Harvard Law School says, "Freedom, much like equality, is an empty concept. . . . Whether freedom is good or bad depends entirely on the particular substantive cause on behalf of which freedom is invoked."[130] Another law professor, Peter Westen, wrote a famous essay in the *Harvard Law Review* entitled "The Empty Idea of Equality," making the same argument.[131] What are they saying?

When we appeal to the principle of freedom we usually mean that people should be free to live as they choose, as long as they don't harm or diminish the freedom of others.[132] The problem with this seemingly simple idea is that it assumes we all agree on what harm is. To use a well-known example, someone might say that it is unjust to have strict obscenity laws, that they constitute a violation of our freedom of speech. No one is forcing the use of "adult" literature and movies on anyone unless they choose to purchase them and use them. "What I do in private doesn't harm anyone" is the justification. In this view, it is unjust to curtail the freedom to produce and use such material, since it does no harm.

However, it could be argued that such a position is sociologically naïve. For one thing, what you do in private shapes the kind of person you become. The movies and literature you use affect how you talk and act, and how you relate to other people. Since you interact with the community, what you do in private does affect others. And besides, if you purchase such materials you create a market for them, and that means they will be available for the children of people who vehemently prefer that they would be inaccessible. So your purchase and use of these things forces some people to live an environment that they do not want for their families. The same situation that you consider "free," others consider an oppressive imposition on them.[133]

Many other examples could be cited. What if you began a new business that competes with mine, and because it is far more efficient and profitable, it will soon drive me into bankruptcy. Could I not claim that you are harming me severely, and that you should be shut down? In America we would say that your new business does not constitute harm, because free enterprise in the long run is better for human flourishing.

However, there are many other cultures that believe otherwise. So freedom is indeed something of an "empty" concept, as Klarman said, because the causes for which freedom is invoked are always matters of deeply held beliefs, rooted in particular views of human nature and happiness and right and wrong that are matters of faith. We all agree that freedom should be curtailed if it harms people, but we can't agree on what harm is, because we have different views of what healthy, flourishing human life looks like.[134]

So it was not helpful for the supporters of the senior female staff member to simply cry "injustice." As Klarman says, you have to discuss the merits of the underlying values for which justice is being invoked. But that conversation never took place among those staffers, and this story is a picture of our society today.

Competing Visions

The philosopher Alasdair MacIntyre has written a book entitled *Whose Justice? Which Rationality?*[135] In the volume MacIntyre lays out the competing visions of justice in our society, which he traces back to thinkers such as Aristotle, Aquinas, and Hume. The best book for revealing how these competing views operate is Harvard law professor Michael Sandel's *Justice: What's the Right Thing to Do?*[136] Sandel lays out three current views of justice, which he calls "maximizing welfare," "respecting freedom," and "promoting virtue."[137] According to one framework, the most just action is that which brings the greatest good to the greatest number of people. According to the second, the most just action is that which respects the freedom and rights of each individual to live as he or she chooses. According to the last view, justice is served when people are acting as they *ought* to, in accord with morality and virtue. These views lead to sharply different conclusions about what is just in particular cases.[138]

Why do we have such gridlock in our society over justice? Underneath all notions of justice is a set of faith assumptions that are essentially religious, and these are often not acknowledged. In an important book, *The Disenchantment of Secular Discourse*, law professor Steven D. Smith reminds us that by the rules of secular discourse that reign particularly in government, politics, and the academy, no one is allowed to ever bring religious beliefs into public argument. We are not supposed to talk about moral rights and moral evils, because that would get us into endless disagreements over which religious faith is the true one. We should only talk about justice in the supposedly neutral terms of freedom and equality that we can all agree on. But as we have seen, this does not work because our ideas of justice are rooted in views of life that are nonprovable faith assumptions. Smith writes:

> The secular vocabulary within which public discourse is constrained to operate today is insufficient to convey our full set of normative convictions and commitments. We manage to debate normative matters anyway—but only by smuggling in notions that are officially inadmissible. . . . The fact that we must smuggle in . . . our real commitments [that we] often cannot articulate . . . even to ourselves—ensures that our discourse will often be barren, unsatisfying, and shallow. . . .[139]

To use a simple example, it is often argued that corporal punishment violates the rights and human dignity of a child, and therefore should be illegal. Smith reminds us, however, that there is no secular, scientific basis for the idea of human dignity, or that human beings are valuable and inviolable. Historian Carl L. Becker famously said that, from a strictly scientific viewpoint, human beings must be viewed as "little more than a chance deposit on the surface of the world, carelessly thrown up between two ice ages by the same forces that rust iron and ripen corn." Scientist Stephen Hawking agrees that "the human race is just a chemical scum on a moderate size planet" and most recently Harvard psychologist Stephen Pinker wrote an essay entitled "The Stupidity of Dignity." The prominent philosopher John Gray, who teaches at the London School of Economics, writes in his book *Straw Dogs: Thoughts on Humans and Other Animals* of the self-deception of those who embrace science and still hold to the tenets of liberal humanism, such as belief in human dignity and rights.[140]

So, concluded Smith, to say that corporal punishment violates a child's dignity and rights seems more objective than to say, "I think corporal punishment of children is morally offensive," but the latter statement is a more frank expression of how you reached your conclusion.[141] The rules of secular discourse lead us to smuggle moral value judgments into our reasoning about justice without admitting it to others or even to ourselves. And so the deeper discussions over the true points of difference never happen.

Sandel gives us another, far more controversial example of this. He says that the most familiar liberal argument for abortion rights "claims to resolve the abortion question on the basis of neutrality and freedom of choice, without entering into the moral and religious controversy."[142] Abortion rights supporters charge that their pro-life opponents are trying to impose a particular set of moral and religious views on society, but that pro-choice people are not. They are simply arguing for freedom of choice. Sandel retorts:

> But this argument does not succeed. For if it's true that the developing fetus is morally equivalent to a child, then abortion is morally equivalent to infanticide. And few would maintain that government should let parents decide for themselves whether to kill their children. So the "pro-choice" position on the abortion debate is not really neutral on the underlying moral and theological question; it implicitly rests on the assumption that the Catholic Church's teaching on the moral status of the fetus . . . is false.[143]

Sandel's point can be further illustrated by reference to the issue of slavery in America. Why did we not give people the freedom to own slaves or not? It was because as a society we made the moral determination that members of all races were fully human. So if our society gives women the freedom to have abortions, it is because we also have made a moral determination. Sandel concludes: "It is not enough to say that the law should be neutral on moral and religious questions. The case for permitting abortion is no more neutral than the case for banning it. Both positions presuppose some answer to the underlying moral and religious controversy."[144]

Sandel, who is not a religious believer and who is a supporter of abortion rights, concludes that justice is always "judgmental."[145] Beneath all accounts of justice are sets of essentially religious assumptions that we are not allowed to admit or discuss, and so our society stays in a deadlock over these issues. We can't agree on what justice is because we can't talk about our underlying beliefs.

Cooperation and Provocation

How should Christians proceed to do justice in this kind of environment? I propose that Christians' work for justice should be characterized by both humble cooperation and respectful provocation.

Christian believers have many temptations to be neither humble nor cooperative with others. Believers have many of the criteria for a righteous and just life laid out in the Bible. How easy it would be to disdain all non-Christian accounts of justice as being useless, just as many secular people dismiss religious belief.

However, Christians' own theology should lead them to appreciate the competing views of justice that Sandel outlines in our society because they know from the Bible that they are all partly right. The utilitarians are concerned with the common welfare. And in the book of Proverbs, we learn that people living justly do not consider their money to belong to them alone, but also to the community around them. Liberals are most concerned with individual rights. And, as we have seen, the Bible gives us the strongest foundation for the idea of rights that there is. According to the Bible, your neighbor comes into your presence with certain claims on you, that you treat him in ways that enhance his well-being, that you don't torture, defraud, or abduct him. Why? Because, as Genesis 9:6 says, he has an inherent worth, an inviolable dignity because he is made in the image of God.

Finally, conservatives believe justice is a matter of giving people what they deserve and of promoting virtue. As Sandel and others have shown, neither the utilitarians' "harm" principle, nor the liberal emphasis on equal rights is sufficient for doing justice. Under the call for freedom and equality is always a set of moral intuitions and value judgments. Christians will heartily agree with this. Biblical guidelines give believers many important insights for determining the kinds of cases Sandel presents. Sometimes Christians will side with one school of thought, other times they will side with another.[146] In other words, according to the Bible, virtue, rights, and the common good are all crucial aspects of justice.

Why should Christians expect that many who do not share their Biblical beliefs will nonetheless want to work for the same goals? The apostle Paul taught that human beings who have never read or known the Bible, nevertheless "show that the requirements of [God's] law are written on their hearts, their consciences also bearing witness" (Romans 2:15). Theologians have called this "general revelation" as contrasted with the "special revelation" of the Bible. God reveals much of his will to human consciences through what has been called "the light of nature."[147] For example, even if someone does not believe the Biblical teaching that God made man in his own image, nevertheless the sacredness and dignity of every human being can be known intuitively, without belief in the Bible.

As a result of this general revelation, Christians believe that that there is much "common grace" in every culture. The implication of James 1:17 is that God scatters gifts of wisdom, goodness, justice, and beauty across all the human race, regardless of people's beliefs.[148] Christians see all skill in science, scholarship, crafts, government, art, and jurisprudence as being from God.[149] This grace is called common because it is given to all, not just those who have found salvation in Jesus Christ, yet this grace "provides the basis for Christians to cooperate with, and learn from, non-Christians," as theologian Richard Mouw points out.[150] In short, the

Bible warns us not to think that only Bible-believing people care about justice or are willing to sacrifice in order to bring it about. As one theologian puts it: "Acts of kindness and self-sacrifice surface among every race and class of human beings, not because we are simple mixtures of good and evil, but because even in the midst of our deep rebellion, God restrains us and displays his glory and goodness."[151]

Christians should realize then some part of society will always recognize some of what the Bible calls "justice." When we speak publicly, we should do so with thoughtfulness and grace, in recognition that Christians are not the only ones who see what needs to be done in the world. We should not simply be quoting the Bible at people. As author Ken Myers says, "When Christians articulate cultural values, they should be values that non-Christians can embrace as well, not because we have some prior commitment to 'pluralism,' and thereby seek to be inoffensive, but because we have expressed values which [because of common grace] are in fact common values."[152]

Christians should identify themselves as believers as they seek justice, welcoming and treating all who work beside them as equals. Believers should let their co-workers know of how the gospel is motivating them, yet also, as Myers says, they should appeal to common values as much as possible.

What we are laying out here is a balance. On the one hand there are Christians who want to work for social reforms, citing only Biblical reasons, and speaking aggressively against those who do not share their religious beliefs. On the other hand there are those who counsel Christians to not seek social justice at all, predicting that such efforts only make Christians more like the world. Instead, they say, Christians should concentrate on only bringing individuals to faith in Christ and building up the church. The former group is too triumphalist, while the latter group is too pessimistic about the possibilities of cultural change and social reform. Theologian Don Carson writes that once we shed utopian dreams of producing a "redeemed culture," we can look at history and acknowledge that it is possible to "improve and even transform some social structures":

> Sometimes a disease *can* be knocked out; sometimes sex traffic *can* be considerably reduced; sometimes slavery *can* be abolished in a region; sometimes more equitable laws *can* foster justice and reduce corruption. . . . In these and countless other ways cultural change is possible. More importantly, doing good to the city, doing good to all people (even if we have special responsibility for the household of faith), is part of our responsibility as God's redeemed people. . . .[153]

We have said that Christians should acknowledge "common grace," that non-Christians share with us common intuitions about the good, the true, and the just. We should appeal to those common values and work alongside our neighbors in an effort to improve justice in society. We should agree that, according to the Bible, all the various views of justice out there in our society are partly right.

But they are also partly wrong. Each of the theories that Sandel outlines makes one of these factors—virtue, rights, or the common good—into a "bottom line" that trumps the other two. However, the Biblical understanding of justice is not rooted in any one of these, but in the character and being of God himself. This means that no current political framework can fully convey the comprehensive Biblical vision of justice, and Christians should never identify too closely with a particular political party or philosophy.

Many churches have uncritically adopted a liberal political agenda, one that has a very expansive view of government. Others adopt a politically conservative approach to justice, one that insists that poverty, at least in America, is not the result of unjust laws, social structures, and racism, but only a matter of family breakdown. As we have seen, the Biblical material is too nuanced and balanced to fit neatly into either of these schemas. And if we tie the Bible too tightly to any particular economic system or set of public policies, it bestows divine authority on that system.

So even as Christians practice humble cooperation with their allies, they should at the same time be respectfully provocative with them, arguing that their models of justice are reductionistic and incomplete.

"Justice Is Inescapably Judgmental"

Why should we do this? Wouldn't it be best to be pragmatic, to just work together and not to talk about how our beliefs are different than those of others who may be interested in the same basic social goals? In the short run that might be less bother, but in the long run it won't be good for our society.

Our society can't come to grips with the underlying beliefs that inform our differing views of justice. Because we insist that all discussions omit any reference to moral or religious beliefs, we cannot talk about *why* we think something is right and just. Sandel has shown that the ideal of "liberal neutrality," which has dominated modern law and jurisprudence for decades—namely that "we should never bring moral or religious convictions to bear in public discourse about justice and rights" [154]—is actually an impossibility. He writes:

> Justice is inescapably judgmental. Whether we're
> arguing about financial bailouts . . . surrogate
> motherhood or same-sex marriage, affirmative
> action or . . . CEO pay . . . questions of justice are
> bound up with competing notions of honor and
> virtue, pride and recognition. Justice is not only
> about the right way to distribute things. It is also
> about the right way to value things.[155]

And "valuing things" is always based on beliefs
about the purposes of life, human nature, right and
wrong—all of which are moral and religious.

The ancient Greek philosophers believed all things
and persons were designed by transcendent forces for a
purpose, a *telos,* and without reference to that *telos* it is
impossible to determine how we should live. For example, imagine I am a person from a very remote part of
the world and I've never seen a cell phone (or a phone,
for that matter). You give it to me, and I immediately
try to pound a stake into the ground with it. It breaks,
of course, and I complain, "This thing you gave me is
no good." You will explain that the cell phone was not
designed for driving stakes into the ground, but for
communicating across distances. Unless you know the
telos of something, what it is *for,* you can't make right
judgments about whether the thing is good or bad.

How do we determine what is good or evil human

behavior? Aristotle and his followers answer: Unless you can determine what human beings are here *for*, you can't answer that.[156]

One of the best examples of what Aristotle argues is the very concept of human rights. Many still believe that the idea of human rights was developed by thinkers of the secular Enlightenment such as Hobbes and Locke. Brian Tierney of Cornell University has demonstrated that, on the contrary, it was within Christian jurisprudence of the twelfth and thirteenth centuries that human rights thinking began, rooted particularly in the Christian doctrine that all human beings are created in the image of God, and therefore have inherent dignity.[157]

We heard from Stephen Hawking, Stephen Pinker, and John Gray that there is no neutral, scientific basis for proving that every human being, regardless of gender, race, age, and ability, has inherent worth. Therefore even atheist and agnostic philosophers acknowledge that the concept of human rights requires a religious dimension. Raimond Gaita has written that when secular thinkers speak of "inalienable rights" they are "trying to make secure to reason what reason cannot finally underwrite," because the idea of human rights has its origin in the concept of "human sacredness," which was born in religious traditions.[158] Even the philosopher Jacques Derrida agrees:

Today the cornerstone of international law is the sacred, what is sacred in humanity. You should not kill. You should not be responsible for a crime against this sacredness, the sacredness of man as your neighbor . . . made by God or by God made man. . . . In that sense, the concept of crime against humanity is a Christian concept and I think there would be no such thing in the law today without the Christian heritage, the Abrahamic heritage, the biblical heritage.[159]

Marxist literary critic Terry Eagleton also resists the efforts of atheist writers such as Richard Dawkins and Christopher Hitchens to devalue the contribution of religion to the maintenance of justice in human society. "The difference between science and theology," Eagleton writes, "is one over whether you see the world as a gift or not."[160] He goes on in his book *Reason, Faith, and Revolution* to argue that it makes an enormous difference to how one lives in the world if you see human beings as accidental beings rather than a sacred creation and gift of God.

This in no way means that nonreligious people cannot believe in human dignity and human rights. Millions of them can and do.[161] But any such belief is, in itself, essentially religious in nature.

A New Conversation

Sandel, Smith, and many others say that we must begin again to talk about moral and religious beliefs in public discourse. The rules of secular public discourse will not allow us to talk about such matters, since, it is feared, discussions of religious beliefs will lead to endless public disagreement. However, we are *already* locked in endless disagreement, largely because we live with the illusion that we can achieve moral and religious neutrality. And because we can't talk about our real differences, we simply make power plays to weaken and marginalize our opponents, not persuade them. We have to change these rules and this climate of discourse. Christians can be an important part of changing this climate from one of yelling "injustice!" to one of talking and seeking justice together.

Another important figure who seems to agree with all this is U.S. president Barack Obama, who has said:

Secularists are wrong when they ask believers to leave their religion at the door before entering into the public square. Frederick Douglass, Abraham Lincoln, William Jennings Bryan, Dorothy Day, Martin Luther King—indeed, the majority of great reformers in American history—were not only motivated by faith, but repeatedly used religious language to argue for their cause. So to say that men and women should not inject their "personal morality" into public policy debates is a practical absurdity. Our law is by definition a codification of morality, much of it grounded in the Judeo-Christian tradition.[162]

There will still be plenty of voices urging Christians to be quiet about their faith in the public square, but these are voices who continue to believe that it is possible to argue for justice on the basis of "neutral, secular reason." That viewpoint may be on the wane.

The pursuit of justice in society is never morally neutral, but is always based on understandings of reality that are essentially religious in nature. Christians should not be strident and condemning in their language or attitude, but neither should they be silent about the Biblical roots of their passion for justice.

EIGHT

PEACE, BEAUTY, AND JUSTICE

*Seek the peace and prosperity of the city to which I
have carried you into exile. Pray to the LORD for it,
because if it prospers, you, too, will prosper.*

Jeremiah 29:7

The Biblical idea of justice is comprehensive and
practical, but it is also high and wonderful. It is
part and parcel of what God is doing in history. God
is reconciling humanity to himself—and as a result of
this great transaction, he is reconciling all things to
himself. He is bringing all things in heaven and earth
together in Christ (Colossians 1:20; Ephesians 1:10).
What does this mean?

The Artwork of God

The Jewish Scriptures were virtually unique in their
view of how the world began. Most other ancient ac-

counts depict creation as the result of a battle or of a struggle between warring cosmic forces.[163]

A Chinese account describes how the primordial giant Pangu emerged from the ancient cosmic egg, and when he died the parts of his body became the world—his eyes the sun and moon, his body the mountains, his blood the waters, his muscles the land, his beard the forests. One African story tells of a giant who got sick and vomited out the world, first the sun, moon, and stars, and then vegetation and human beings. The Gnostics taught that the high God was unknowable, and in contradiction to God's will, some lower deity, a "demiurge," created the profoundly flawed material world. In Norse mythology the god Odin killed the giant Ymir and used his body to create the universe and its inhabitants. The Babylonian account, the *Enuma Elish,* tells a similar story of the god Marduk who defeats the ocean goddess Tiamat and produces the world out of her members.

In most ancient myths, therefore, the visible universe resulted from conflict, powers in tension with one another. The Biblical creation account, however, stands in stark contrast. Biblical scholar Gerhard von Rad has argued that, unlike any of its neighbors, Israel could conceive of no divine powers on a par with those of the Lord.[164] Creation was therefore the work of God without a rival, who made the world not as a warrior digs a trench but as an artist paints a picture or shapes a sculpture. God is a craftsman, an artisan.

A House and a Garment

Sometimes the imagery the Bible uses to describe creation is architectural. God says to Job: *"Where were you when I laid the earth's foundation. . . . [and] marked out its dimensions?"* (Job 38:4–6). In the beginning, God built the world to be not only our home but his royal dwelling (Isaiah 66:1). In the Psalms we learn that when he built the world it had to have, as does any house, a foundation, and that foundation was "righteousness and justice." Jewish scholar Moshe Weinfeld says, "This refers to the imposition of equality, order, and harmony upon the cosmos and the elimination of the forces of destruction and chaos."[165] God brought order out of chaos, as a builder takes a pile of raw materials and rightly relates them to one another in order to form a house.

The Bible describes the making of the world not only as the building of a house, but also as the weaving of a garment. God turned a chaos into a cosmos, and also turned a tangle into a tapestry. Woven garments were long in the making and valuable in ancient times, and therefore they were an apt metaphor for the wonder and character of the material world. The sea (Psalm 104:6), the clouds (Job 38:9), the lights of the sky (Psalm 104:1), and all the forces of nature (Psalm 102:26) are called garments that God has woven and now wears.

As a result, the world is not like a lava cone, the product of powerful random eruptions, but rather like a *fabric*. Woven cloth consists of innumerable threads interlaced with one another. Even more than the architectural image, the fabric metaphor conveys the importance of *relationship*. If you throw thousands of pieces of thread onto a table, no fabric results. The threads must be rightly and intimately related to one another in literally a million ways. Each thread must go over, under, around, and through the others at thousands of points. Only then do you get a fabric that is beautiful and strong, that covers, fits, holds, shelters, and delights.

God created all things to be in a beautiful, harmonious, interdependent, knitted, webbed relationship to one another. Just as rightly related physical elements form a cosmos or a tapestry, so rightly related human beings form a community. This interwovenness is what the Bible calls shalom, or harmonious peace.

Forms of Shalom

"Shalom" is usually translated "peace" in English Bibles, but it means far more than what our English word conveys. It means *complete* reconciliation, a state of the fullest flourishing in every dimension—physical, emotional, social, and spiritual—because all relationships are right, perfect, and filled with joy.[166]

When your body is healthy, especially when you are young, you have energy, strength, and beauty, because all the parts of your body are working in unity. But when you are injured, parts of your body may be out of alignment with others. Cancer cells work not with but against the other systems of the body. When the parts of your body fail to work interdependently, you experience the loss of physical shalom or well-being. And when you die, you literally unravel.

When you experience a season of mental well-being, it is because the things your emotions want are those of which your conscience and reason approve. Your inner faculties are working together. However, you may find yourself longing intensely for something that your reason tells you is futile or your conscience tells you is absolutely wrong, but you can't stop wanting it or seeking it. Then you experience an inner unraveling of psychological shalom, commonly given names like "guilt," "being conflicted," or "anxiety."

Then there is social shalom. In the Frank Capra movie *It's a Wonderful Life,* George Bailey and his family run a savings and loan company in the small town of Bedford Falls, New York. Over the years they had helped innumerable families get mortgages at fair and reasonable rates, and had been patient and caring when loans couldn't be repaid. As the CEO of his company, George's "bottom line" was not maximum profits, but the flourishing of his community and customers. George, of course, did not get rich with this kind of approach! But at one point in the movie, when he is suicidal, he is given a vision of what Bedford Falls would have looked like if, as he wished at the moment, he "had never been born." What he sees is a community consisting of some wealthy families surrounded by an impoverished, dysfunctional town. Instead of kindly neighbors, there are brutal and self-interested parties in constant conflict with one another. Without George Bailey's efforts the town had lost its social shalom.

When the society disintegrates, when there is crime, poverty, and family breakdown, there is no shalom. However, when people share their resources with each other, and work together so that shared public services work, the environment is safe and beautiful, the schools educate, and the businesses flourish, then that community is experiencing social shalom. When people with advantages invest them in those who have fewer, the community experiences civic prosperity or social shalom.

Losing Shalom

But the world is not, by and large, characterized by shalom. How did we get into this place? The beginning of the book of Genesis tells us how in the Garden of Eden, humanity walked with God and served him. Under his rule and authority, it was paradise. We know something of this on a mundane level. Excellent managers can take over unprofitable businesses or losing sports franchises and, through their leadership skills, turn everything around. Under new, competent authority morale builds, the conflicts end, the team jells, vision is recaptured, and everyone thrives. This is just a dim hint of what happens under the absolute reign of the true and living God. All things reach their potential and flourish in perfect harmony.

All that ended, however, when humanity turned away from God, rejecting his rule and kingdom. The third chapter of Genesis spells out the results in comprehensive detail. Sin entered the world to deface and mar everything that had been made. Because we became estranged from God, we also are alienated from our true selves, and from each other. Our primal self-absorption has led to profound social evil—to war, crime, family breakdown, oppression, and injustice. When we lost our relationship with God, the whole world stopped "working right." The world is filled with hunger, sickness, aging, and physical death. Because our relationship with God has broken down, shalom is gone—spiritually, psychologically, socially, and physically.

Justice and Shalom

Now we are in a position to see even more clearly what the Bible means when it speaks of *justice*. In general, to "do justice" means to live in a way that generates a strong community where human beings can flourish. Specifically, however, to "do justice" means to go to places where the fabric of shalom has broken down, where the weaker members of societies are falling through the fabric, and to repair it.[167] This happens when we concentrate on and meet the needs of the poor.

How can we do that? The only way to reweave and strengthen the fabric is by weaving your*self* into it. Human beings are like those threads thrown together onto a table. If we keep our money, time, and power to ourselves, for ourselves, instead of sending them out into our neighbors' lives, then we may be literally on top of one another, but we are not interwoven socially, relationally, financially, and emotionally. Reweaving shalom means to sacrificially thread, lace, and press your time, goods, power, and resources into the lives and needs of others.

An intriguing real life example of an entire community doing justice and seeking shalom is laid out in Yale professor Nora Ellen Croce's book *Everyone Here Spoke Sign Language*.[168] In the 1980s Croce was researching hereditary deafness on Martha's Vineyard. In the seventeenth century the original European settlers were all from a region in Kent, England, called "the Weald" where there was a high incidence of hereditary deafness. Because of their geographical isolation and intermarriage the percentage of deaf people increased across the whole island. By the nineteenth century one out of twenty-five people in the town of Chilmark was deaf and in another small settlement almost a quarter of the people could not hear.[169] (Today, because of the mobility of the population and marriage with off-islanders, hereditary deafness has vanished. The last deaf person born on the Vineyard died in 1952.)

In most societies, physically handicapped people are forced to adapt to the life patterns of the nonhandicapped, but that is not what happened on the Vineyard. One day Croce was interviewing an older island resident and she asked him what the hearing people thought of the deaf people. "We didn't think anything about them, they were just like everyone else," he replied. Croce responded that it must have been necessary for everyone to write things down on paper in order to communicate with them. The man responded in surprise, "No, you see everyone here spoke sign language." The interviewer asked if he meant the deaf people's families. No, he answered, "Everybody in town—I used to speak it, my mother did, everybody." Another interviewee said, "Those people weren't handicapped. They were just deaf."[170] One other remembered, "They [the deaf] were like anybody else. I wouldn't be overly kind because they, they'd be sensitive to that. I'd just treat them the way I treated anybody."[171]

Indeed, what had happened was that an entire community had disadvantaged itself en masse for the sake of a minority. Instead of making the nonhearing minority learn to read lips, the whole hearing majority learned signing.[172] All the hearing became bilingual, so deaf people were able to enter into full social participation. As a result of "doing justice" (disadvantaging themselves) the majority "experienced shalom"—it included people in the social fabric who in other places would have fallen through it. "When they had socials or anything up in Chilmark, why, everybody would go and they [the deaf] enjoyed it, just as much as anybody did. They used to have fun—we all did. . . . They were part of the crowd, they were accepted. They were fishermen and farmers and everything else. . . . Sometimes, if there were more deaf people than hearing there, everyone would speak sign language—just to be polite, you know."[173] Deafness as a "handicap" largely disappeared.

Perhaps the most interesting aspect of Croce's research was the revelation of how hearing people had their own communication abilities enhanced. They found many uses for signing besides communication with the deaf. Children signed to one another during sermons in church or behind a teacher's back at school. Neighbors could sign to one another over distances in a field or even through a spyglass telescope. One woman remembers how her father would be able to stand on a windy cliff and sign his intentions to fishermen below. Another remembers how sick people who could not speak were able to sign to make their needs known.[174]

In other words, the "disadvantage" that the hearing Vineyarders assumed—the effort and trouble to learn another language—turned out to be for their benefit after all. Their new abilities made life easier and more productive. They changed their culture in order to include an otherwise disadvantaged minority but in the process made themselves and their society richer.

Martha's Vineyard was a unique situation. However, in every time and culture, the principle holds. The strong must disadvantage themselves for the weak, the majority for the minority, or the community frays and the fabric breaks.

Justice and Beauty

In 1999 Harvard English professor Elaine Scarry wrote a book in which she took on the prevailing view of the late twentieth century academy, namely, that beauty and attractiveness was the handmaiden of privilege, masking political power interests. On the contrary, she said in the book with a title that conveys its main thesis—*On Beauty and Being Just.* Beauty, she asserted, can lead us to a more just life. Her first argument was that the observer of beauty always receives a passion to share the beauty with others. This serves as "an introduction (perhaps even our first introduction) to the state of certainty."[175] Beauty, she says, gives us the unavoidable conviction, even if we intellectually have no "metaphysical referent" for it, that life is not random and meaningless, that there is good and evil. We want to share that experience with others, to have others praise and enjoy the beauty with us.[176]

Her second argument was that beauty radically "decenters" the self and moves you to distribute attention away from yourself. She quotes philosopher and author Iris Murdoch's famous lecture "The Sovereignty of Good over Other Concepts," in which Murdoch describes once having been absorbed in anxiety and self-pity, but then she looked out a window to see a bird riding the thermals.

We are anxiety-ridden animals. Our minds are continually active, fabricating an anxious, self-preoccupied, falsifying veil which partially conceals the world. . . . [But] I am looking out of my window in an anxious and resentful state of mind, brooding on some damage done to my prestige. Then suddenly I observe a hovering kestrel. In a moment everything is altered. The brooding self with its hurt vanity has disappeared. . . . And when I return to thinking of the other matter it seems less important. . . .[177]

Scarry observed that, in Murdoch's experience, the new vision of beauty occupied "all the space formerly in the service of protecting, guarding, advancing the self" (or its prestige). In the presence of beauty you cease to be the hero in your own story. It is no longer all about you. You experience a "symmetry of everyone's relation to one another."[178]

Theologian Jonathan Edwards, in his book *The Nature of True Virtue*, argued that human beings will only be drawn out of themselves into unselfish acts of service to others when they see God as supremely beautiful.[179] Here's an example to illustrate what he means. If you listen to the music of Bach because you want people to think you are cultured (or because you want to think it of yourself), then the music is only a

means to achieve some other end, namely the enhance-
ment of your reputation. But if you play Bach because
you find it not just useful but beautiful, then you are
listening to it as satisfying in and of itself.

Edwards taught that if, through an experience of
God's grace, you come to find him beautiful, then you
do not serve the poor because you want to think well
of yourself, or in order to get a good reputation, or
because you think it will be good for your business, or
even because it will pay off for your family in creating
a better city to live in. You do it because serving the
poor honors and pleases God, and honoring and pleas-
ing God is a delight to you in and of itself.

Scarry and Murdoch are not making anything like
Edwards's appeal to the beauty of God as the basis for
just living. And yet together they acknowledge that
there is an obstacle to doing justice in human nature
that will not be removed simply through education,
argument, and persuasion. It takes an experience of
beauty to knock us out of our self-centeredness and
induce us to become just.

Columbia professor Todd Gitlin reviewed Elaine
Scarry's book and was not convinced by it. Quoting
George Steiner, he observed that the Nazis slaugh-
tered people by day and enjoyed Mozart by night.[180]
Edwards taught that "secondary beauty," such as the
beauty of art, may have some humbling, decenter-

ing effect, since all beauty is derived from God. But I'm sure he would have agreed with Gitlin that such beauty is insufficient to produce justice. There is, however, one supreme kind of beauty that will.

God in the Face of the Poor

Proverbs 19:7 and 14:31 are texts that sum up a great deal of Scriptural material. The first text says that if you are kind to the poor, God takes it as if you are being kind to him. The second gives us the flip side; namely, that if you show contempt for the poor it means you are showing contempt for him.

One of the more notorious practices of local banks is to "redline" poor and nonwhite neighborhoods. That is, they refuse mortgage and small business loans to applicants who live there. Their argument is that they simply look at the statistics and conclude that residents of those neighborhoods are more likely not to make good on the loan. God, however, says we are not to live that way in our relationships to the poor. He says, in effect, in Proverb 19:7: "Don't *you* dare 'redline' people. Don't look at someone and say, 'If I get involved with that person I might be taken advantage of!' I see a gift to the poor as a gift to me. I will, in some way, make the loan good. I will give you value, trust me."

This is not a promise to match literal dollars for dollars, but to enrich your life and meet your needs (Mark 10:29–31). What a promise that is! In your life you may already have family members, friends, or neighbors who have chronic problems and who are difficult to love. And out in your community there are more. Don't shrink, says the Lord, from spending yourself on the broken, the hurting, and the needy. I'm good for it.

But there's a deeper principle at work here. If you insult the poor, you insult God. The principle is that God personally identifies very closely with the widow, the orphan, and the immigrant, the most powerless and vulnerable members of society. When the Old Testament says God identifies with the poor, that is a strong statement. But it still is basically a figure of speech. Not until you come to the New Testament can you fully grasp the degree to which God has done this.

In Proverbs we see God identifying with the poor symbolically. But in the incarnation and death of Jesus we see God identifying with the poor and marginal literally. Jesus was born in a feed trough. When his parents had him circumcised the offering they made— two pigeons—was that prescribed for the poorest class of people in the society.[181] He lived among the poor and the marginalized, who were drawn to him even as the respectable were repulsed by him. We see the kind of life he led when he said, "Foxes have holes, birds have nests, but the Son of Man has nowhere to lay his head" (Luke 9:58). At the end of his life he rode into Jerusalem on a borrowed donkey, spent his last evening in a borrowed room, and when he died he was laid in a borrowed tomb. They cast lots for his only possession, his robe, for there on the cross he was stripped of everything. He died naked and penniless. He had little the world valued and the little he had was taken. He was discarded—thrown away. But only because of Him do we have any hope.

In Jesus Christ God identified not only with the poor, but also with those who are denied justice. Dr. James Montgomery Boice once preached a sermon entitled "The Illegalities of Christ's Trial."[182] Examining the account of Jesus's trial before the Sanhedrin in John 18 he listed all the ways that the trial was a miscarriage of justice: There was no public notification; it was held in middle of the night; Jesus was allowed no defense; he was forcibly struck in the middle of the trial. Later the colonial governor, Pontius Pilate knew the case was insufficient but he caved in to political pressure. Finally, Jesus was tortured cruelly and put to death. In all these ways, Jesus identifies with the millions of nameless people who have been wrongfully imprisoned, robbed of their possessions, tortured, and slaughtered.

Many people say, "I can't believe in God when I see all the injustice in the world." But here is Jesus, the Son of God, who knows what it's like to be the victim of injustice, to stand up to power, to face a corrupt system and be killed for it. He knows what it is like to be lynched. I'm not sure how you believe in a God remote from injustice and oppression, but Christianity doesn't ask you to believe in that. That is why the Christian writer John Stott is able to say, "I could never myself believe in God if it were not for the Cross. In the real world of pain, how could one worship a God who was immune to it?"[183]

And what does this mean? Remember Matthew 25. On the last day Jesus sits on the judgment seat, saying:

> *"For I was hungry and you gave me food, I was thirsty and you gave me drink, I was a stranger and you welcomed me, I was naked and you clothed me, I was sick and you visited me, I was in prison and you came to me."*
>
> *Then the righteous will answer him, saying, "Lord, when did we see you hungry and feed you, or thirsty and give you drink? And when did we see you a stranger and welcome you, or naked and clothe you? And when did we see you sick or in prison and visit you?"*
>
> *And the King will answer them, "Truly, I say*

to you, as you did it to one of the least of these my
brothers, you did it to me."

Matthew 25:35–40

On Judgment Day, don't say to the Lord, "When did we see you thirsty, naked, and captive?" Because the answer is—on the cross! There we see how far God was willing to go to identify with the oppressed of the world. And he was doing it all for us! There Jesus, who deserved acquittal and freedom, got condemnation—so that we who deserve condemnation for our sins can receive acquittal (Galatians 3:10–14; 2 Corinthians 5:21). This was the ultimate instance of God's identification with the poor. He not only became one of the actually poor and marginalized, he stood in the place of all those of us in spiritual poverty and bankruptcy (Matthew 5:3) and paid our debt.

Now *that* is a thing of beauty. To take *that* into the center of your life and heart will make you one of the just.

Some years ago I heard a man relate the experience of a wealthy older woman that he once knew.[184] She had never married and had no children to serve as heirs. She had only one close relative, a nephew, who hoped to inherit her money. He had always been gracious and attentive in her presence, but she had heard things from others that made her doubt her impression. The disposal of her wealth was no small matter. She had to be sure that the person who received it would use it wisely and generously. So she decided to take matters into her own hands. One morning she dressed in tattered clothes, appearing to be a homeless person, and lay on the steps of his urban town house. When he came out, he cursed at her and told her to leave or he would call the police. And so she knew what his heart was really like. His response to the poor woman revealed his true nature.

Proverbs 14:31 says, "He who oppresses the poor shows contempt for their Maker." The God of the Bible says, as it were, "I *am* the poor on your step. Your attitude toward them reveals what your true attitude is toward me." A life poured out in doing justice for the poor is the inevitable sign of any real, true gospel faith.

NOTES

INTRODUCTION – **Why Write This Book?**

1. The Corporation for National and Community Service is
   an independent agency of the U.S. government, created
   to support community service and volunteerism, and the
   publisher of *Volunteering in America*. The article from
   which the quotes in this paragraph are taken is by Mark
   Hrywna, "Young Adults Fueled Spike in Volunteers," in
   The NonProfit Times, July 28, 2009, accessed at http://
   www.nptimes.com/09Jul/bnews-090728-1.html.
2. Ibid.
3. See Walter Rauschenbusch, *A Theology for the Social Gospel* (New York: Macmillan, 1922), chapter 19, "The Social
   Gospel and the Atonement," where Rauschenbusch rejects
   the theory of penal substitution and sees Jesus's death as
   revealing the social injustice of this world, as well as the
   sacrificial, unselfish generosity that must be our operating
   principle if we are to heal the world of its evil.
4. Jonathan Edwards, "Christian Charity: The Duty of Charity to the Poor, Explained and Enforced," in vol. II of *The
   Works of Jonathan Edwards*, ed. Sereno Dwight (Carlisle,
   Pa.: Banner of Truth Trust, 1998), p. 164.
5. It might be objected that Jonathan Edwards was speaking here of only charity to the poor, not justice. But for

Edwards, the word "charity" meant more than what we use it to mean today. See more on Edwards's views in other chapters.

6. See Amy Sullivan, "Young Evangelicals: Expanding their Mission" in *Time*, June 1, 2010. Accessed at http://www.time.com/time/printout/0,8816,1992463,00.html on July 10, 2010. Sullivan writes: "Today's young Evangelicals cut an altogether different figure. They are socially conscious, cause-focused, and controversy-averse. And they are quickly becoming a growth market for secular service organizations like Teach for America. Overall applications to Teach for America have doubled since 2007 as job prospects have dimmed for college graduates. But applications have tripled from graduates of Christian colleges and universities. Wheaton is now ranked sixth among all small schools—above traditionally granola institutions like Carleton College and Oberlin—in the number of graduates it sends to Teach for America. The typical Wheaton student, like many in the newest generation of Evangelicals, is likely to be on fire about spreading the Good News and doing good."

7. An example is Joel B. Green and Mark D. Baker, *Recovering the Scandal of the Cross* (Downers Grove, Ill.: Inter-Varsity, 2000.)

8. Christopher Hitchens, *God Is Not Great: How Religion Poisons Everything* (New York: Hatchette, 2007).

9. "Jeffrey" (not his real name) was one of the brightest students in the school. When he graduated from high school, all other students with his grades got into private or Ivy League schools. He could not afford that, and went to a very inexpensive state school. Nevertheless, he went on to get a Ph.D. and today teaches in one of the premier graduate schools in the country.

Notes

10. See Brian Tierney, *The Idea of Natural Rights: Studies on Natural Rights, Natural Law, and Church Law 1150–1625* (Grand Rapids, Mich.: Eerdmans, 1997). See chapter 1. See also chapter 2, "A Contest of Narratives," in Nicholas Wolterstorff, *Justice: Rights and Wrongs* (Princeton: Princeton University Press, 2008).

11. David L. Chappell, *A Stone of Hope: Prophetic Religion and the Death of Jim Crow* (Chapel Hill: University of North Carolina Press, 2004). Also, see Richard W. Willis, *Martin Luther King, Jr., and the Image of God* (New York: Oxford University Press, 2009.). This book argues that King and the African-American church drew heavily on the Biblical account that all humans are made in "the image of God" and are therefore equal and must be treated with dignity.

12. Some of the results of this work can be found in my book *Ministries of Mercy: The Call of the Jericho Road* (Grand Rapids: Zondervan, 1986).

13. Harvie M. Conn, *Evangelism: Doing Justice and Preaching Grace* (Grand Rapids: Zondervan, 1982).

14. Elaine Scarry, *On Beauty and Being Just* (Princeton: Princeton University Press, 1999).

ONE – What Is Doing Justice?

15. The Scripture quotations in this book are ordinarily taken from the New International Version translation. Sometimes I provide my own translations. The NIV, for example, regularly renders the word *gare* as "alien," whereas I will usually translate it "immigrant," which, I think, more accurately conveys to modern readers the meaning of the word. The word means "the outsider living in your midst."

16. Mark Gornik now heads up City Seminary of New York in

Notes

New York City. I consider Mark's ministry to be an excellent, instructive example of how to do justice in a poor community. His book, *To Live in Peace: Biblical Faith and the Changing Inner City* (Grand Rapids: Eerdmans, 2002), is an important theological reflection on the work of justice, particularly in a city. We will return to Mark's work in chapter 2, where we hear his analysis of what makes a neighborhood poor, and in chapter 6, where I give an overview of the balanced system of ministries that Mark and others developed in Baltimore.

17. See Peter Craigie, *Twelve Prophets, Volume 2: Micah, Nahum, Habakkuk, Zephaniah, Haggai, Zechariah, and Malachi* (Philadelphia: Westminster, 1985). "Although we may learn deeply from each of the three parts of the prophet's message, it is the collective whole which is most vital" (p. 47). See also Bruce K. Walke, *A Commentary on Micah* (Grand Rapids: Eerdmans, 2007), p. 394.

18. Waltke, *Micah*, p. 394.

19. This is a term coined, from what I can tell, by Wolterstorff, p. 75.

20. Howard Peskett and Vinoth Ramachandra, *The Message of Mission: The Glory of Christ in All Time and Space* (Downers Grove, Ill.: InterVarsity Press, 2003), p. 113. Also quoted in Tim Chester, *Good News to the Poor: Sharing the Gospel through Social Involvement* (Nottingham, UK: InterVarsity Press, 2004), p. 19.

21. The main source of this term is Gustavo Gutiérrez, *A Theology of Liberation: History, Politics, and Salvation* (Maryknoll, N.Y.: Orbis, 1973). It is now available in a fifteenth anniversary edition from Orbis, publication date 1988.

22. Nicholas Wolterstorff, *Justice: Rights and Wrongs* (Princeton: Princeton University Press, 2008), p. 79.

Notes

23. Ibid.

24. Christopher Wright, *Deuteronomy* (Exeter, UK: Paternoster, 1996), p. 13.

25. J. A. Motyer, *The Prophecy of Isaiah: An Introduction and Commentary* (Downers Grove, Ill.: InterVarsity Press, 1993), p. 471.

26. These are Wolterstorff's terms, and I think they are more positive and descriptive than the more common labels. Rectifying justice is usually named "retributive" justice (that is, punishing wrongdoers and reestablishing rights) and primary justice is usually called "distributive" justice (that is, making sure that goods and opportunities are more equitably distributed in society).

27. Christopher Wright sums it up nicely: "*Mishpat* is what needs to be done in a given situation if people and circumstances are to be restored to conformity with *tzadiqah.*" *Old Testament Ethics for the People of God* (Downers Grove, Ill.: InterVarsity Press, 2004), p. 237.

28. Francis I. Anderson, *Job: Tyndale Old Testament Commentary* (Downers Grove, Ill: InterVarsity Press, 1975), p. 231.

29. The metaphor of a father helping his children is useful in several aspects. A good father gives his children direct aid—he feeds them and protects them from danger. But a good father does not want his children to remain dependent on him forever. He wants them to grow up and become self-sufficient. So, too, helping the poor may begin with direct relief and protection, but the final goal should always be empowerment and self-sufficiency. To keep the poor dependent is paternalistic and unloving, and ultimately unjust.

30. Wright, *Old Testament Ethics*, p. 257.

31. "[This text] is careful to not define righteousness merely

in negative terms. It is not enough simply not to be a robber. The righteous person is actively generous. It is not
enough to say, as one often hears in situations of bereave-
ment, 'He never did anyone any harm.' The question one
is tempted to ask is, 'Yes, but did he ever do anyone any
good?'" Christopher J. H. Wright, *The Message of Ezekiel*
(Downers Grove, Ill.: InterVarsity Press, 2001), p. 194.

TWO – Justice and the Old Testament

32. Craig Blomberg, *Neither Poverty Nor Riches: A Biblical
    Theology of Possessions* (Downers Grove, Ill.: InterVarsity
    Press, 1999), p. 39.
33. Christopher Wright, *Deuteronomy* (Carlisle, UK: Paternos-
    ter, 1996), p. 188.
34. A perennial question is, though believers in the Old Tes-
    tament were required to tithe their income, are New Testa-
    ment Christians so required? The principle we have been
    using—that the coming of Christ changes Old Testament
    laws, yet they still have some abiding validity—holds true
    for tithing. In Luke 11:42 Jesus chastises the Pharisees
    for "tithing your garden herbs . . . but neglecting justice
    and the love of God." That is, they were diligent to tithe
    their income, but they were exploitative in their business
    dealings and unjust in their relationships. Then Jesus adds,
    "You should have practiced the latter without leaving the
    former undone." In other words, Jesus affirms tithing, but
    says that by itself it is not enough. Put another way, for
    a Christian, tithing is a *minimum* standard for generosity
    and doing justice. Christian believers are not less indebted
    to and blessed by God than Old Testament believers were.
    Therefore we should not imagine that God's standards
    for generosity would be lower for New Testament Chris-

tians than for Old Testament believers. "To whom much is given, much shall be required"(Luke 12:48).

35. There is some debate about whether this was an additional tithe in the third year (thus a 20 percent donation that year!) or whether this meant only that the single third-year tithe was distributed this way. We know that by the time of Josephus (a Jewish writer who lived after the time of Christ) the Jews practiced not only two tithes in the third year but an additional "third of a tithe" special offering for the poor, which brought the individual family's giving that year to 23.3 percent. See Blomberg, pp. 46ff, and Wright, pp. 183–186.

36. Modern readers are often offended by the very fact that the Mosaic Law allowed slavery at all. One friend once said to me, "It's nice that God commanded that the slaves be set free every seven years, but why did he allow slavery in the first place?" However, an Old Testament Israelite slave was more like an "indentured servant" than what we would call a "slave" today. When an Israelite fell into slavery, it was a temporary condition, because of indebtedness. Slavery through kidnapping and trafficking in Israel was punishable by death (Deuteronomy 24:7, cf. 1 Timothy 1:9–11). Also, you could not mistreat a slave, because if you even knocked out his tooth he was to be set free (Exodus 21:27).

Most interesting of all is the remarkable passage Deuteronomy 23:15–16, which directs: "If a slave has taken refuge with you, do not hand him over to his master. Let him live wherever he likes. . . . Do not oppress him." This is a direct contradiction of all existing slave laws of other societies in both ancient and modern times. Slave laws always penalized runaway slaves as well as those who harbored them. What does this law mean? Bible scholar Chris Wright proposes two implications. First, if this refers to all Israelite slaves, it assumes that experience of slavery in Israel was not so harsh that there would be a great number of runaways. Indeed, Deuteronomy 15:16ff allows a slave to voluntarily remain in servitude after the Sabbath year, which indicates that many opted for this. A runaway slave, then, could be presumed to be someone who was being mistreated. "When reading the Old Testament, we need to put out of our minds pictures of slavery derived from Roman galley slaves or more recent black slavery because these are quite inappropriate analogies for what a slave was in Israel." Wright, *Deuteronomy*, p.249.

Even if this law referred to only runaway *foreign* slaves (rather than to Israelite slaves), this indicates a major, "intentional critique of the very nature of the institution [slavery] itself. That is, the legal rights and expectations intrinsic to slavery as a social institution are subordinated to the rights of the slave as a human being with needs. . . . In this case, the needs of the weaker party (the slave seeking refuge) are given explicit legal preference over the claims of the stronger (the master seeking his return)" (p.250). In other words, the owner's economic investment in the slave is relative to the absolute moral obligation to treat the slave as a human being with dignity. Wright concludes: "This Deuteronomic law on slavery is pointing in a direction that ultimately undermines slavery itself" (p.250).

37. Blomberg, p. 45.
38. Blomberg, p. 46.
39. See chapter 4 for some thoughts by Jonathan Edwards on this condition.
40. A Biblical example is in 2 Kings 4:1–7, where a woman loses her husband and cannot pay her debts, and stands to become homeless because of a merciless creditor. The natural disaster—the loss of her husband—left her defenseless

before powerful economic forces. She was saved only when God stepped in and, through the prophet Elisha, miraculously multiplied a single jar of oil into a large inventory, which she sold to eliminate her debt. Other Biblical characters who stepped in to defend disaster victims against the ruthless include Boaz (Ruth 4) and Job himself (Job 29 and 31).

41. Two *New York Times* op-ed pieces show that more thinkers are coming to this nuanced, balanced, complexified view of poverty. See Orlando Patterson, "A Poverty of Mind," in *The New York Times*, March 25, 2006, and also "Jena, O.J., and the Jailing of Black America," *The New York Times*, September 30, 2007. See also Henry Louis Gates, Jr., "Forty Acres and a Gap in Wealth" in *The New York Times*, November 18, 2007.

42. Mark R. Gornik, *To Live in Peace: Biblical Faith and the Changing Inner City* (Grand Rapids: Eerdmans, 2002), p. 40.

43. Ibid., pp. 42–43.

44. See especially William Julius Wilson, *When Work Disappears: The World of the New Urban Poor* (New York: Alfred Knopf, 1996).

45. I knew a minister who moved with his family into a poor neighborhood, and soon afterward his wife applied to get a new credit card. She was instantly turned down, despite having a normal middle-class credit history. It was simply because of her new address.

46. Ibid., pp. 54–57.

47. Robert A. Caro, *The Power Broker: Robert Moses and the Fall of New York* (New York: Vintage, 1975).

48. For more on the practical multidimensionality of doing justice in a neighborhood, see chapter 6.

49. D. Carson, R. T. France, J. Motyer, G. Wenham, eds., *New*

Notes

Bible Commentary: 21st Century Edition (Downers Grove, Ill.: InterVarsity Press, 2000), p. 129.

THREE – What Did Jesus Say About Justice?

50. Anders Nygren, *Agape and Eros*, translated by Philip S. Watson (London: SPCK, 1953), p. 70. Quoted by Nicholas Wolterstorff in *Justice: Rights and Wrongs* (Princeton: Princeton University Press, 2008), p. 100. On pp. 98–108 Wolterstorff summarizes and refutes Nygren's argument that in the Bible justice and love are complete incompatibles.

51. See D. A. Carson, *The Gospel According to John* (Leicester, UK: InterVarsity Press, 1991), p. 227.

52. John Newton, *The Works of John Newton*, Volume 1 (Carlisle, Pa.: Banner of Truth edition, 1985), p. 136.

53. In what way did the scribes denounced in Mark 12:40 and Luke 20:47 "devour widows' houses"? The gospel texts do not explain. Scholars have proposed several ideas. One possibility is that temple authorities and clergy were often entrusted with the management of the property of elderly widows, and they may have routinely done so in a way that enriched the managers and impoverished the widows by charging exorbitant fees. There are references in the Talmud that speak of this practice. See Darrell L. Bock, *Luke, Volume 2:9:51–24:53* (Grand Rapids: Baker, 1996), pp. 1643–1644, for a full treatment.

54. While the term "neglecting justice" could sometimes mean to break the law, in the context it clearly means that they are not showing care or concern for the poor. Every commentator I was able to consult, of every theological perspective, agrees that the term "justice" here has to do with the Old Testament concept of loving and defending the vulnerable.

Notes

55. Joel B. Green, *The Gospel of Luke* (Grand Rapids: Eerdmans, 1997), p. 471.

56. There is controversy over whether "my brethren" are Christians or not. It seems to me that they are, since that word is never used by Jesus in the gospels to refer to anyone but those who recognize him as the Christ. So this is a call to create a believing community in which the well-off and middle class are sacrificially giving their resources away and deeply, personally involved in the lives of the many weak and vulnerable in their midst. Readers who are disappointed that this does not speak to how Christians are to relate to the poor of the world, beyond the believing community, should look at the Good Samaritan parable and other passages that instruct Christians to not limit their social concern to only believers (e.g., Galatians 6:10). Some interpreters have pressed further and said that these "brethren" to be received are really evangelists, and therefore Jesus is saying that, though they are poor, people should listen to their message. This seems to me to be unlikely. Some of these brethren are in prison and sick—not likely to be traveling evangelists. And, as we have seen, Jesus's language is close to that of Isaiah 58. He is reasserting the prophetic challenge for Christians to create a community of justice in which the well-off share what they have with poorer brethren.

57. See D. A. Carson, *The Expositor's Bible Commentary: Matthew Chapters 13 through 28* (Grand Rapids: Zondervan, 1995). "The reason for admission to the kingdom in this parable is more evidential than causative. This is suggested by the surprise of the righteous in verses 37–39" (p. 521).

58. Harvie Conn, *Bible Studies in Evangelization and Simple Lifestyle* (Carlisle, UK: Paternoster, 1981), p. 18.

Notes

59. In Acts 5, there is an account of two members of the early church—Ananias and Sapphira—who gave a generous gift, claiming to have donated the whole proceeds from the sale of a piece of property. In reality, they held back some of the income for themselves. As a result of this lie God judged them and they died. Because of the dramatic results, one implication of the passage is often overlooked. In the early church, radical generosity was so important and valued that people were prepared to fake it.

60. "It cannot be accidental that Luke, in his portrayal of the beginnings of the . . . community of the Holy Spirit, chose to describe them in words taken almost directly from the LXX [the Greek] translation of verse 4, simply changing its future tense to the past. ("There were no needy persons among them," Acts 4:34). C. Wright, *Deuteronomy*, p. 189.

61. Some people will be surprised that, in my survey of Jesus's teaching on justice, I do not treat the important subject of "the kingdom of God." Indeed, many consider this the main theme of Jesus's ministry, and most writers who expound the Biblical teaching on justice constantly invoke it. I have not done so for several reasons. One is that there is so little consensus among Christian thinkers about the precise meaning of the term. Most agree that God's kingdom is his redemptive reigning power, that it was inaugurated by Jesus at his first coming into the world and will be brought to completion at his second coming. But as to the exact nature of that kingdom and how it manifests itself today there is much disagreement. Some understand it more individualistically, that it is a spiritual realm we enter when we are converted, so that now God is ruling in our hearts and bringing about changes in our lives. Others understand it more corporately. They see the kingdom as

[202]

a set of new social arrangements, or as the healing of broken relationships between people of different classes and races. Those who take this view believe the kingdom of God is a way that God brings about changes not just in individual lives, but in the world and society. They believe, for example, that when Christians help the poor, they are therefore doing "kingdom work," but others would disagree with them, and would insist that only evangelizing and discipling—building up the Body of Christ—is "kingdom work." An overlapping issue is the debate about the relationship of the present and future worlds. Is this physical world going to be completely burned up and replaced by a new heavens and new earth, or will the present world be renewed, cleansed, and healed? If the former is the case, then all that matters is saving souls, since everything on this earth is going to burn up anyway.

As you can see, the issues are complex, and the space I have in this book is limited, so I have proceeded by showing that an extremely strong case for doing justice and caring for the poor can be made without entering into debates over the nature of the kingdom and other matters of "eschatology." As we will discover in chapter five, Jonathan Edwards was able to make an extremely strong case for ministry to the poor from the central, traditional doctrines of penal substitution, redemption, and salvation by grace. Having said that, I believe the kingdom of God has a corporate aspect. "Blessed are the poor," Jesus said (not merely the "poor in spirit"), "for yours is the kingdom of God" (Luke 6:20). There in Luke 6:20ff, Jesus taught that, while the world's system valued power ("you who are rich"), material comfort ("you who are well fed"), success ("you who gloat"), and recognition ("you when all men speak well of you"), members of his kingdom did not make these things into life goals or priorities. A community of people who, instead, lives for service, embrace of the "Other," and is characterized by sacrificial giving—will inevitably create a "counterculture," a new social arrangement unlike that of the world. Also, Luke 6:20–35 must mean (at least) that now the brokenhearted, the unrecognized, and the oppressed have a central place in the heart and life of the people of God. I have written more on the relationship of the kingdom of God to justice and evangelism in "The Gospel in All Its Forms," which can be found online at http://www.christianitytoday.com/le/2008/spring/9.74.html.

FOUR – **Justice and Your Neighbor**

62. I should note here that, in general, I believe that the local church's "diaconal" funds should be mainly used to help people with needs who are members or who are involved in the church's worship and community life. In order to reach the poor of the city and the world, it is best—for both practical and theological reasons—to organize Christian nonprofits and other institutions to do that. I will discuss this more in chapter 6.

63. This paragraph is based on the account of Mark Valeri, *Works of Jonathan Edwards: Sermons and Discourses, 1730–1733*, vol. 17 (New Haven: Yale University Press, 1999), p. 22.

64. The sermon can be found in Valeri, *Works of Jonathan Edwards, 1730–1733*, vol. 17, pp. 369ff. But there are also some versions of this sermon that are on the Internet in numerous places.

65. Some might point out that Edwards was speaking here of only charity to the poor, not justice. However, Edwards

in this sermon was reminding the economically prosperous in his congregation that their social standing was a gift of undeserved grace. A lack of generosity to the poor was not, then, just stinginess, but injustice. Edwards insisted that public charity to the indigent was not enough, that Christians should aim for the complete eradication of poverty in their civic community, and that not to give generously, far past the minimum survival-only-level of public welfare, was a sin. See Gerald McDermott, *One Holy and Happy Society: The Public Theology of Jonathan Edwards* (State College: Pennsylvania State University Press, 1992), p. 160. Edwards also attacked businessmen who took advantage of market conditions to gain exorbitant profits at the expense of the poor. (See Edwards's sermon "Dishonesty: or the Sin of Theft and Injustice," in *Works of Jonathan Edwards*, vol. 2, E. Hickman, ed. (Carlisle, Pa.: Banner of Truth edition, 1974), p. 222. From these examples we see that Edwards had a keen understanding of "primary" or social justice—of the rights of the poor and the obligations of others to lift them up. For Edwards, a lack of "charity" was a sin, and therefore a violation of God's law and justice.

66. Edwards in Valeri, p. 395.
67. Ibid., p. 394.
68. Ibid., p. 398.
69. Ibid., p. 397.
70. Ibid, p. 401.
71. Ibid, p. 402.
72. Ibid.

FIVE – Why Should We Do Justice?

73. Arthur Allen Leff, "Unspeakable Ethics, Unnatural Law," *Duke Law Journal*, December 1979.

Notes

74. Richard Rorty, "Human Rights, Rationality, and Sentimentality," in Stephen Shute and Susan Hurley, eds., *On Human Rights: The Oxford Amnesty Lectures 1993* (New York: Basic Books, 1993), pp. 133–134.

75. From a letter to Frederick Pollock, in Richard Posner, ed., *The Essential Holmes* (Chicago: University of Chicago Press, 1992), p. 108.

76. C. S. Lewis, *The Weight of Glory and Other Addresses* (New York: HarperCollins, 2001), p. 46.

77. A very important book discerning the different ways the Bible speaks of God's love is Don Carson, *The Difficult Doctrine of the Love of God* (Leicester, UK: InterVarsity Press, 1999). Carson shows that neither a very conservative view ("God loves only those who are saved") nor a very liberal view ("God loves all people without distinction") does justice to the nuanced Biblical doctrine of the love of God.

78. Wolterstorff, *Justice: Rights and Wrongs*, pp. 357–359.

79. Aristotle, *Politics*, book I, part V. The quote is taken from the translation by Benjamin Jowett (Mineola, N.Y.: Dover Thrift Edition, 2000), p. 12.

80. Preached at Ebenezer Baptist Church, Atlanta, Georgia, July 4, 1965. It was accessed online on March 30, 2010, at http://teachers.marisths.org:81/mhs_oldham/amdream .pdf.

81. C. S. Lewis, *The Weight of Glory*, p. 46.

82. Bruce K. Waltke, *The Book of Proverbs: Chapters 1–15* (Grand Rapids: Eerdmans, 2004), p. 96. Also see Waltke's article "Righteousness in Proverbs," in *Westminster Theological Journal* 70 (2008): 207–24.

83. Christopher Wright, *Deuteronomy*, p. 261.

84. The importance of this line of reasoning is seen in its repetition. God says repeatedly that his redemption of his

Notes

people is the basis for "doing justice." The case is repeated in Deuteronomy 24:17–22: "Do not deprive the alien or the fatherless of justice. . . . Remember that you were slaves in Egypt and the LORD your God redeemed you from there."

85. I take a traditional reading of Paul, despite the fact that over the last twenty-five years there have been many who have moved away from this classic Protestant interpretation of him. This move away from Luther and Calvin has been called the "New Perspective on Paul." For the simple summary (and good brief critique) of the NPP see Simon Gathercole, "What Did Paul Really Mean?" in *Christianity Today,* August 2007. Accessed on April 10, 2010 at http://www.christianitytoday.com/ct/2007/august/13.22.html.

86. Martin Luther "Preface" in *Commentary on Paul's Epistle to the Galatians* (Cambridge, UK: James Clarke, 1953), pp. 25–26. I have modernized some of the language.

87. A traditional problem is how to reconcile the fact that James says, "We are not justified by faith alone," while Paul says that we are "justified by faith alone." The answer is—"James and Paul use 'justify' to refer to different things. Paul refers to the initial declaration of a sinner's innocence before God; James to the ultimate verdict of innocence pronounced over a person at the last judgment. While a sinner can get into relationship with God only by faith (Paul), the ultimate validation [proof] of that relationship takes into account the works that true faith must inevitably produce (James)." D. Moo, *The Letter of James,* pp. 141–142. For more on James's teaching on the relationship of grace and justice, see chapter five.

88. D. A. Carson, *The Expositors Bible Commentary: Matthew Chapters 1 to 12* (Grand Rapids: Zondervan, 1995), p. 132. See also R. T. France, *The Gospel of Matthew*

Notes

(Grand Rapids: Eerdmans, 2007), pp. 164–65. France writes: "'Poverty in spirit' [speaks] of a person's relationship to God. It is a positive spiritual orientation, the converse of the arrogant self-confidence which not only rides roughshod over the interests of other people but more importantly causes a person to treat God as irrelevant." On the parallel passage "the poor and contrite in spirit" (Isaiah 66:2), Alec Motyer writes that the term means "a sense of inability in spiritual matters . . . helplessness to please God." Motyer, *The Prophecy of Isaiah*, p. 534.

89. This essay is a chapter in Miroslav Volf, *Against the Tide: Love in a Time of Petty Dreams and Persisting Enmities* (Grand Rapids: Eerdmans, 2010) pp. 137–139.

90. Ibid., p. 138.

91. *Sermons of M'Cheyne* (Edinburgh: n.p., 1848). I use this text and make similar arguments in chapter 3 of an earlier book, *Ministries of Mercy: The Call of the Jericho Road*, 2nd ed. (Phillipsburg, N.J.: Presbyterian and Reformed Publishing Co., 1997).

SIX – How Should We Do Justice?

92. See the additional commentary on this text given on it in chapter 1.

93. See Derek Kidner, *Psalms 1–72: An Introduction and Commentary* (Downers Grove, Ill.: InterVarsity Press, 1973), p. 161.

94. This is simply from the Wikipedia entry for "Business Ethics." It is a good example of the typical lines of reasoning in courses and discussion on corporate ethics. See en.wikipedia.org/wiki/business_ethics.

95. Bruce K. Waltke, *The Book of Proverbs: Chapters 1–15*, p. 96.

Notes

96. One way that many Christians seek to do justice in their daily life and work is by paying attention to the sources of the products they consume. In a 1995 article, reporter Bob Herbert tells of visiting a factory in El Salvador that made jackets for Liz Claiborne. While the jackets sold in the U.S. for $178 each, workers got 77 cents per jacket. A female worker being interviewed after her twelve-hour shift revealed that while desperate to keep the job, her low wages made it impossible for her to even buy milk for her three-year-old daughter. The U.S. clothing companies are simply "shopping around the whole world for the cheapest labor price."(Bob Herbert, "In Maquiladora Sweatshops: Not a Living Wage," *Minneapolis Star Tribune*, October 22, 1995.) Catholic theologian William T. Cavanaugh recounts Herbert's article, and then contrasts Liz Claiborne with the Spanish worker-owned manufacturing company, the Mondragón Cooperative Corporation. Mondragón, really a federation of worker cooperatives, is based on the idea that if labor hires capital, the economic arrangements will be more just than when capital hires labor. In Mondragón, the highest-paid employee, on average, can make no more than five or six times what the lowest-paid make; 10 percent of surpluses are given directly to community development projects. Mondragón currently employs over ninety-two thousand workers, and studies have shown that the communities in which Mondragón employs many people are unusually healthy. (William T. Cavanaugh, *Being Consumed: Economics and Christian Desire* [Grand Rapids, Mich.: Eerdmans, 2008], pp. 16–17). Christians who want to support justice in the world may wish to patronize some companies over others. I would add that this whole area is fraught with difficult questions. Many argue that even the low wage jobs created by U.S. companies overseas

give an enormous boost to national economies, and that free enterprise in the long run lifts the interests of both labor and capital. Some Christian thinkers are far more positive about the morality of free markets than others.

97. "Mary" is a pseudonym and I also changed details to preserve her anonymity.

98. Wright, *Deuteronomy*, p. 261.

99. The stories of these ministries are told vividly by Perkins in books such as *A Quiet Revolution* (Waco, Tex.: Word, 1976), *Let Justice Roll Down* (Ventura, Calif.: Regal, 2006), *Restoring At-Risk Communities* (Grand Rapids: Baker, 1996), *Beyond Charity: The Call to Christian Community Development* (Grand Rapids: Baker, 1993).

100. Charles Marsh and John M. Perkins, *Welcoming Justice: God's Movement toward Beloved Community* (Downers Grove, Ill.: InterVarsity Press, 2009), p. 25. See also Marsh's *The Beloved Community: How Faith Shapes Social Justice, from the Civil Rights Movement to Today* (New York: Perseus Books, 2005).

101. Marsh and Perkins, p. 30.

102. Some prefer to speak of "reneighboring" rather than mere "relocation." Often, more well-off people move into a poorer neighborhood for two reasons: for cheaper rents or prices on real estate, and/or because living in gritty inner city neighborhoods is considered cool and hip. When many people relocate for these reasons, the result is a spiraling "gentrification," which pushes up rents and pushes the needy out of their community. Reneighboring means to come in carefully, aware of the impact of one's presence on the environment, looking to be a genuine participant and servant of the community, an influence on the common good of the community.

103. Ibid., p. 23.

Notes

104. John Perkins, *With Justice for All* (Ventura, Calif.: Regal, 1982), pp. 146–166.
105. Gornik, p. 129. He points out that the very term "development" has overtones of paternalistic control, but "it still has value."
106. Marsh and Perkins, p. 30.
107. Mishnah (Sanhedrin 10.5), quoted in J. Daniel Hays, *From Every People and Nation: A Biblical Theology of Race* (Downers Grove, Ill.: InterVarsity Press, 2003), p. 50n.
108. Hays, p. 60.
109. What Peter learns in Acts 10:34 is that God does no prosopolempsia. That is, he does not discriminate on the basis of race or class. (See also Ephesians 6:9.)
110. Richard Lovelace, *The Dynamics of Spiritual Life*, (Downers Grove IVP, 1979) p. 199.
111. Needless to say, the subject of racial reconciliation is complicated and filled with many sub-issues. One is the question of whether white Americans today need to repent for the sins of ancestors and acknowledge the white privilege they have today. First, questions about individual and corporate guilt arise. The Bible does speak of repenting and taking some responsibility for the sins of ancestors. (See Daniel 9.) And yet, passages like Ezekiel 18 argue forcefully that individuals will be judged for their own sins only, not the sins of their forbears. It is important to keep both of these truths in balance. Second, your understanding of the causes of poverty will influence your practice of racial reconciliation. If you believe that African-American poverty is mainly the result of systemic racism and exclusion, or if you think it is almost completely caused by a breakdown in family and personal responsibility, it will influence your whole approach to racial unity and reconciliation. For

Notes

a balanced, conservative survey of the different approaches to racial justice and reconciliation, see John Piper's forthcoming *Bloodlines: Race, Cross, and the Christian*. For an account that puts much emphasis on the systemic nature of racism, see Emmanuel Katongole and Chris Rice, *Reconciling All Things: A Christian Vision for Justice, Peace, and Healing* (Downers Grove, Ill.: InterVarsity Press, 2008).

112. See www.bostontenpoint.org.

113. In Israel, under the Mosaic legislation, all sacrifices to God were offered at the central sanctuary—the tabernacle and later the temple—by the priests. Job was his family's priest (Job 1:4–5), and this means that the events in the life of Job evidently did not occur within the boundaries of the theocratic nation-state of Israel.

114. Robert Linthicum, *City of God, City of Satan: A Biblical Theology of the Urban Church* (Grand Rapids: Zondervan, 1991), pp. 45–47.

115. Ibid.

116. Many items on this list are taken from a survey done by the International Justice Mission in 1996 of seventy Christian ministries serving globally in missions, relief, and development. See Gary Haugen, *Good News About Injustice* (Downers Grove, Ill.: InterVarsity Press, 2002), p. 41.

117. LaVerne S. Stokes, "Preface" to Mark Gornik, *To Live in Peace*, p. xiii.

118. Gornik quoting from *Christianity, Social Change, and Globalization in the Americas* (New Brunswick, N.J.: Rutgers University Press, 2001), in Gornik, p. 13.

119. All quotes on this page are taken from Gornik, pp. 12–13.

120. There is far more to do to prepare and mobilize a church for doing justice. Years ago I wrote a more practical manual

Notes

for this, and it contains many more details than are laid out here. See Timothy J. Keller, *Ministries of Mercy: The Call of the Jericho Road*, 2nd ed. (Phillipsburg, N.J.: Presbyterian and Reformed Publishing Co., 1997), chapters 8 through 14. See also Amy Sherman, "Getting Going: Ten Steps to Building a Community Ministry," in *Restorers of Hope* (Wheaton, Ill.: Crossway, 1997). Another book that is helpful for people asking, "Where can I start with doing justice?" is Mae Elise Cannon, *Social Justice Handbook: Small Steps for a Better World* (Downers Grove, Ill.: Inter-Varsity Press, 2009). This book gives numerous modest "small first steps" for beginning to do justice. Two books on Christian community development and community organizing are Robert Linthicum's *Empowering the Poor* (Federal Way, Wash.: World Vision International, 1991) and *Transforming Power: Biblical Strategies for Making a Difference in Your Community* (Downers Grove, Ill.: InterVarsity Press, 2003). Also see Shane Claiborne, *The Irresistible Revolution: Living as an Ordinary Radical* (Grand Rapids: Zondervan, 2006). All these books will give you a host of practical ideas for doing justice in your community. However, I must attach a note to them. The divergent theories of justice in our society are very powerful, and Christian authors are usually influenced by one of them or the other. Some of these books will assume a more conservative, individualistic theory of justice and others the view that poverty is almost completely the result of unjust social systems. And you, the reader, will also be influenced by these theories. So, for example, if you are a political conservative you will find little objectionable in Amy Sherman's book but you will have much to object to in Linthicum's books. I propose that readers remember that the Biblical concept of justice is very comprehensive and therefore it should be possible to glean great ideas from all kinds of sources.

121. Also see 2 Thessalonians 3:10: "If a man will not work, he shall not eat." A text like this must be balanced with a text like Acts 4:32 where it is said that "anyone" who had a need was helped. We must help anyone in the church in need, but if we love them, and they are acting irresponsibly, we must keep their feet to the fire in some way so that they begin to change their ways. See Jonathan Edwards's thoughts on how to help "the undeserving poor" in chapter 4.

122. An example of this point of view is C. P. Wagner, in his book *Church Growth and the Whole Gospel* (New York: Harper and Row, 1981), pp. 101–104.

123. Quoted in James I. McCord, ed., *Service in Christ* (Grand Rapids: Eerdmans, 1966).

124. For an excellent account of how generosity and care for the poor were crucial to the evangelism of the early church, see Alan Kreider, "They Alone Know the Right Way to Live" in Mark Husbands and Jeffrey P. Greenman's *Ancient Faith for the Church's Future* (Downers Grove, Ill.; InterVarsity Press, 2008). Kreider notes that early Christianity grew explosively—40 percent per decade for nearly three centuries—at a time when "early Christians did not engage in public preaching; it was too dangerous. There were practically no evangelists or missionaries whose name we know. . . . The early Christians had no mission boards. They did not write treatises on evangelism. . . . The worship services of the early Christians . . . after Nero's persecution in the mid-first century . . . closed their worship services to visitors. Deacons stood at the churches' doors, serving as bouncers, checking to see that no unbaptized

person, no "lying informer," could come in. . . . And yet
the church was growing. Officially it was a *superstition*.
Prominent people scorned it. Neighbors discriminated
against the Christians in countless petty ways. Periodi-
cally the church was subjected to pogroms. . . . It was hard
to be a Christian. . . . And still the church grew. Why?"
(pp. 169–170). This striking way of laying out the early
church's social situation forces us to realize that the church
must have grown only because "it was attractive. People
were fascinated by it, drawn to it as to a magnet" (p. 170).
Kreider goes on to make a strong historical case that what
attracted nonbelievers was the Christians' concern for the
weak and the poor, their economic sharing, and their sacrificial love even for their enemies.

125. See Irene Howat and John Nicholls, *Streets Paved with
Gold: The Story of London City Mission* (Fearn, Scotland:
Christian Focus, 2003).

126. For a sympathetic overview of Kupyer's view, see Daniel
Strange, "Evangelical Public Theology: What on Earth?
Why on Earth? How on Earth?," pp. 58–61, in Chris
Green, ed., *A Higher Throne: Evangelical Public Theology*
(Nottingham, UK: InterVarsity Press, 2008).

127. See Daniel Strange, pp. 52–57. The issue of how the church
relates to culture is a crucial and vast subject, well beyond
the scope of this book. Strange outlines two alternative
views. First, he discusses the "Two Kingdoms" view, which
insists neither the church as an institution nor individual
Christians should seek directly to reform society according
to the Biblical vision for justice. Second, he discusses the
"Transformationist" view, often associated with Abraham
Kuyper, which calls Christians to work in the world "from
a distinct Christian worldview" and so to transform cul-

Notes

ture. Strange points out the dangers of both but in the end chooses a moderate version of the Transformationist model. See also note 149.

128. Here we come to two important theological debates: The first is the debate about the nature of the church's "mission," namely, is the mission of the church only to preach the Word—evangelizing and making disciples—or is it also (or mainly) to do justice? Increasingly, evangelicals are talking about the church's "justice mission." See Amy L. Sherman, "The Church on a Justice Mission" in *Books and Culture*, July/August 2010. In this article examples are given of local evangelical congregations that have added the combating of sex/human trafficking to their churches' mission work. Indeed, sex trafficking is an important justice issue and an easy one for most evangelical churches to get a handle on. Nevertheless, I am of the opinion that Kuyper is right: It is best to speak of the "mission of the church," strictly conceived, as being the proclamation of the Word. More broadly conceived, it is the work of Christians in the world to minister in word and deed and to gather together to do justice.

SEVEN – Doing Justice in the Public Square

129. In some cases, a more appropriate term than "allies" is the term "cobelligerents." This refers to groups who are sharply opposed on most other issues but who agree to work in tandem on one particular issue where they agree. An example might be radical feminists working with fundamentalists to oppose pornography.

130. Michael J. Klarman, "Rethinking the History of American Freedom," *William and Mary Law Review*, vol. 42 (Fall 2000), pp. 265, 270.

Notes

131. Peter Westen, "The Empty Idea of Equality," *Harvard Law Review*, vol. 95, no. 3 (1982), p. 537.

132. This extremely influential principle was originally proposed by John Stuart Mill in his essay "On Liberty," where he wrote, "The sole end for which mankind are warranted, individually or collectively, in interfering with the liberty of action of any of their number, is . . . to prevent harm to others." Quoted in Steven D. Smith, *The Disenchantment of Secular Discourse* (Cambridge: Harvard University Press, 2010), p. 70.

133. This example is taken from Smith, *Disenchantment*, pp. 84–86.

134. See chapter 3, "Trafficking in Harm," in Smith, *Disenchantment*, pp. 70ff.

135. Alasdair MacIntyre, *Whose Justice? Which Rationality?* (Notre Dame, Ind.: Notre Dame University Press, 1988).

136. Michael Sandel, *Justice: What's the Right Thing to Do?* (New York: Farrar, Straus and Giroux, 2009).

137. Sandel, *Justice*, p. 6.

138. Here are two cases that Sandel uses to show how different accounts of justice lead to different verdicts on cases. One case has to do with price gouging after Hurricane Charley in 2004, when many businesses in Florida raised their prices enormously on basic housing repair materials. There was an outcry and Florida enforced laws against price gouging. But this touched off a debate about whether price gouging laws were just. On the one side people insisted that, even if people were willing to pay the prices, it was greedy and wrong of retailers to charge those amounts. On the other side were many who argued that the gouging laws violated the freedom of producers to set prices at whatever level they could. To prevent this denied a fundamental right in a democratic society. And further, they ar-

gued, only if prices were allowed to rise could manufacturers afford to produce the much greater quantities of their products that the homeowners of Florida needed. Sandel points out that the case ". . . divides ancient and modern political thought. . . . Aristotle teaches that justice means giving people what they deserve. . . . By contrast, modern political philosophers—from Immanuel Kant in the eighteenth century to John Rawls in the twentieth century—argue that the principles of justice that define our rights should not rest on any particular conception of virtue, or of the best way to live. Instead, a just society respects each person's freedom to choose his or her own conception of the good life" (Sandel, *Justice*, p. 8). A more sensational case was that of the English ship the *Mignonette*, which sank during a storm in 1884. Four sailors escaped to a lifeboat, but three survived their weeks at sea only by killing and eating one of their number—a young cabin boy with no parents, spouse, or children, who seemed to be dying anyway. When they returned home to go to trial, the majority of the British public was opposed to their conviction. The young sailor's death had been imminent anyway, they reasoned, and if he had not died others would have been widowed and orphaned. It was better for one to die than that many die and be bereft. If you believe that the justice is primarily the greatest good for the greatest number, then what the sailors did was just. If, however, you believe justice is primarily about individual freedom, then the sailors certainly did an injustice to the young man, because they killed him without his consent. Sandel skillfully shows how these cases divided people because our Western society does not have a consensus definition of justice. Different groups come to different conclusions because each theory has a different "bottom line" for justice.

Notes

139. Smith, *Disenchantment*, p. 39.

140. All these are quoted by Smith, *Disenchantment*, on p. 179.

141. Smith, *Disenchantment*, p. 181.

142. Sandel, *Justice*, p. 251.

143. Ibid.

144. Sandel, *Justice*, p. 252.

145. Sandel, *Justice*, p. 281.

146. Christians have a lot of resources in the Bible to help them make hard decisions about how to live justly in the cases like those cited by Sandel and recounted in Endnote 137. 1. Price gouging after the hurricane. In Leviticus 25:35ff it is forbidden to charge interest on loans to people or even to sell food for profit to those who have fallen into poverty through some disaster. The Mosaic law says that when disaster strikes, we should lower our usual prices for the sake of the victims. We should not make money off of their misfortune. In Florida, a balance would have to have been struck. For most people, prices should go up somewhat so that manufacturers are able produce more needed materials. In a truly just society, the less hard-hit homeowners would be gladly willing to pay higher prices for the sake of the more hard-hit who would pay lower ones. The fact that this is unlikely tells us much about the human heart and why justice is often so scarce. Rather than price gouging laws, which depressed the supply of housing materials, far more special provisions should have been made for low-income people or those hit hardest by the hurricane. Those provisions could have been set in place by both government and private agencies. 2. What about the incident of the *Mignonette*? The reason so many people in Britain thought the sailors had done the right thing is because in the "maximizing welfare" approach to justice, the cabin boy's life was assessed as ultimately less valuable to the hu-

man community. It would have been wrong, in this reasoning, to kill a man with children or a spouse. But the Bible sees all human beings made in the "image of God" to be of equal value. In the Biblical view, gradations of worth based on economic and social factors are not sufficient to measure human value or dignity. The sailors should have done what they could to preserve his life and not treated him as a less valuable commodity. They should have guarded his life and taken their chances, rather than putting themselves in the place of God.

147. Psalm 19 tells us that nature wordlessly "speaks" to us of God. The early parts of the psalm are considered as teaching about general revelation, while the latter half of the psalm praises the Scripture, or "special revelation." In Romans 1:20 Paul reconfirms what Psalm 19 says, but adds the implication that therefore, all human beings are "without excuse" when they disobey what they know of God and his will.

148. For support for reading James 1:17–18 this way, see Ralph P. Martin, *Word Biblical Commentary: James* (Nashville: Word, 1988), pp. 37–42, and Douglas J. Moo, *The Letter of James* (Grand Rapids: Eerdmans, 2000), p. 78. Moo writes: "James, therefore, cites God's creation of the heavenly bodies as evidence of his power and continuing care for the world."

149. A striking example is Isaiah 28:23–29: "When a farmer plows for planting . . . when he has leveled the surface . . . does he not plant wheat in its place, barley in its plot, and spelt in its field? His God instructs him and teaches him the right way. . . . Grain must be ground to make bread . . . all this also comes from the Lord Almighty, wonderful in counsel and magnificent in wisdom." This is remarkable. Isaiah tells us that anyone who becomes a skillful farmer,

Notes

or who brings an advancement in farming "science" is being taught by God. One writes about this text: "What appears as a discovery (the proper season and conditions for sowing, farm management, rotation of crops, etc.) is actually the Creator opening his book of creation and revealing his truth." Alec Motyer, *The Prophecy of Isaiah* (Downers Grove, Ill.: InterVarsity Press, 1993), p. 235. This is a Biblical example of common grace.

150. Richard Mouw, *He Shines in All That's Fair: Culture and Common Grace* (Grand Rapids: Eerdmans, 2010), p. 14.

151. D. A. Carson, *Christ and Culture Revisited* (Grand Rapids: Eerdmans, 2008), p. 49.

152. Ken Myers, "Christianity, Culture, and Common Grace," p. 43, accessed May 31, 2010, at www.marshillaudio.org/resources/pdf/ComGrace.pdf. This essay should be read beside Richard Mouw's *He Shines in All That's Fair: Culture and Common Grace*. The two works give extensive Biblical documentation of the doctrine of common grace, and use it to strongly urge Christians not only to build up the church through evangelism and discipleship, but also to be deeply involved in cultural activity, as philosophers, art critics, filmmakers, journalists, social theorists. They both argue that, without a strong understanding of common grace, Christians break into two extreme camps. First, there are those who become triumphalistic and reestablish "Christendom," seeking to reform culture according to a Biblical blueprint. The other extreme is withdrawal from culture. Both assume that God is not giving nonbelievers any wisdom, insight, or knowledge of truth. In the end, Mouw and Myers draw somewhat different practical conclusions from the doctrine. But even the differences are helpful and instructive.

153. Carson, *Christ and Culture Revisited*, p. 218. Carson points

out that Christians who withdraw from any concern for social justice in the world can fall into an unbalanced version
of Luther's "Two Kingdoms" model of how Christians relate to the culture. This approach insists not only that the
institutional church should not seek any social reform in
the name of Christ, but that even Christians do not engage
in the world—in politics, civil society, academics, or community development—in a distinctively Christian manner.
Their work in the world strictly appeals to common values
that are understood by all because of common grace. This
"Two Kingdoms" approach certainly does eliminate the
utopian triumphalism of some elements of the Christian
Right, but it leads to an opposite error, a form of "quietism." Carson quotes Lutheran Robert Benne: "Were this
version of Lutheran theology taken to its logical conclusion it would deprive the gospel of any intellectual content
and the [civil] law of any moral content. The biblical narrative and theological reflection on it would not be given any
epistemological status to engage secular learning. It would
champion a form of Lutheran quietism in the realm of
education. Much as German Lutherans in the 1930s separated the two kingdoms (government under law separated
from Christianity under the gospel) and allowed the Nazi
movement to go unchecked by appeal to the intellectual
and moral content of the Christian vision, so this approach
would allow modern secular learning to go unchallenged
by that vision." (Quoted on p. 212 of Carson.)

Carson critiques both the triumphalism that can come
from Kuyper's model of relating Christ to culture and the
quietism that can come from Luther's model, as does Dan
Strange (see note 126). While Strange leans more toward Kuyper, Carson comes down in the very middle,
asking for a balance, though also arguing that both these

Notes

models have strengths such that, at different times and places, Christians might draw more on one model than the other. For another very balanced view, written not by a theologian or a Biblical scholar but a Christian sociologist, see James Hunter, *To Change the World: The Irony, Tragedy, and Possibility of Christianity in Late Modernity* (New York: Oxford University Press, 2010). Hunter critiques both opposing views at some length, plus a third, assimilationist model, and proceeds to put forth what he calls "faithful presence." In the end, Strange, Carson, and Hunter all recommend a chastened approach that engages culture but without the triumphalism of transformationism. All of them also insist that the priority of the institutional church must be to preach the Word, rather than to "change culture."

154. Michael Sandel, *Justice*, p. 248.

155. Ibid., p. 261.

156. For a good summary of the Aristotelian understanding of justice, see Sandel's accessible chapter 8—"Who Deserves What? / Aristotle"—in *Justice*.

157. The main book is Brian Tierney, *The Idea of Natural Rights: Studies on Natural Rights, Natural Law, and Church Law 1150–1625* (Atlanta: Scholars Press, 1997). Also see Brian Tierney, "The Idea of Natural Rights—Origins and Persistence," *Northwestern Journal of International Human Rights*, Volume 2 (Spring 2004).

158. Quoted in Michael J. Perry, *Toward a Theory of Human Rights: Religion, Law, Courts* (New York: Cambridge University Press, 2006), p. 18.

159. Jacques Derrida, "On Forgiveness: A Roundtable Discussion with Jacques Derrida," moderated by Richard Kearny, in *Questioning God* (Bloomington: Indiana University Press, 2001), p. 70.

Notes

160. Terry Eagleton, *Reason, Faith, and Revolution: Reflections on the God Debate* (New Haven: Yale University Press, 2009), p. 37.

161. Nevertheless, while it is obvious that plenty of nonbelievers in God can believe in human rights and work very passionately for justice, it is another thing to hold that their belief in rights is intellectually warranted. It can be argued that belief in human rights makes far more sense if there is a God than if there is not. Nicholas Wolterstorff makes this case in "Is a Secular Grounding of Human Rights Possible?" and "A Theistic Grounding of Human Rights," chapters 15–16, in his book *Justice: Rights and Wrongs.* Also see Christian Smith, "Does Naturalism Warrant a Moral Belief in Universal Benevolence and Human Rights?" in J. Schloss and M. Murray, eds., *The Believing Primate: Scientific, Philosophical, and Theological Reflections on the Origin of Religion* (New York, Oxford: Oxford University Press, 2009), pp. 252ff.

162. Barack Obama, "Call to Renewal Keynote Address," Washington, D.C., June 28, 2006, www.barackobama.com/2006/06/28/call_to_renewal_keynote_address.php, quoted in Sandel, p. 246.

EIGHT – Peace, Beauty, and Justice

163. A good brief compilation of ancient creation myths can be found in the Encyclopedia Britannica Online at http://www.britannica.com/EBchecked/topic/142144/creation-myth.

164. Gerhard von Rad, *Wisdom in Israel* (London: SCM Press, 1970), p. 304.

165. Moshe Weinfeld, *Social Justice in Ancient Israel and in the Ancient Near East* (Minneapolis: Fortress, 1995), p. 20.

Notes

Quoted in Christopher J. H. Wright, *Old Testament Ethics for the People of God* (Downers Grove, Ill.: InterVarsity Press, 2004), p. 265, n. 16. Old Testament scholar Bruce K. Waltke also confirms this link between justice and the orderedness of the physical world. He writes that justice is living in accordance with "a universal world order that existed from the creation, [that] manifests itself in the realms of law, wisdom . . . and is guaranteed by God" (quoting H. H. Schmid). He also writes that justice is "to bring about right and harmony for all, for individuals, related in the community and to the physical and spiritual realms. It finds its basis in God's rule of the world" (quoting J. W. Olley). *The Book of Proverbs: Chapters 1–15*, p. 96.

166. See article on "Peace" in *The Dictionary of Biblical Imagery*, L. Ryken, T. Longman, eds. (Downers Grove, Ill.: InterVarsity Press, 1995), p. 632. Or see virtually any other dictionary on Biblical Hebrew terms. For example: "Shalom describes a comprehensive kind of fulfillment or completion, indeed of a perfection in life and spirit which quite transcends any success which man alone, even under the best of circumstances, is able to attain." "Shalom and the Presence of God," in *Proclamation and Presence*, J. I. Durham and J. R. Porter, eds. (Richmond: John Knox, 1970), p. 280.

167. The standard Hebrew lexicon by Koehler and Baumgartner traces the lexical range of the term *mishpat* as "ruling> legal decision, judgment> case> law, right, claim. What is due someone. . . ." (L. Koehler, W. Baumgartner, et al., *The Hebrew and Aramaic Lexicon of the Old Testament*, tr. M. E. J. Richardson, et al. [Leiden: Brill, 1994–99], 2:615). In other words, *mishpat* can mean a legal ruling in a case, or, more basically to the condition that the complainant ought to be in, the treatment that he or she is

Notes

"due." Further, G. Liedke says that in an act of *mishpat* "two people, or groups of people, whose inter-relationship is not intact, are restored to the state of shalom. . . . [*Mishpat*] is a constant preservation of the shalom." (In *Theological Lexicon of the Old Testament*, 3 vols., E. Jenni and C. Westerman, eds., tr. M. E. Biddle [Peabody, Mass: Hendrickson, 1997], 3:1394.) In short, *mishpat* upholds and preserves shalom, the state of complete human flourishing and well-being in every dimension. We will take up this subject again in chapter 2.

168. Nora Ellen Groce, *Everyone Here Spoke Sign Language: Hereditary Deafness on Martha's Vineyard* (Harvard, 1985).

169. In the nineteenth century, 1 American in every 5,728 was born deaf, but on the Vineyard the figure was 1 in every 155 (Groce, p. 3). In Chilmark, the most isolated of the Vineyard towns, the incidence was 1 in 25. About 15 of the 350 people in town were deaf. Most of them lived in a small neighborhood outside Chilmark, where a quarter of the inhabitants were deaf (Groce, p. 42).

170. Groce, pp. 2–3.

171. Groce, p. 51. A woman who married into the Chilmark community in the 1930s said, "I learned it from . . . Abigail [who was deaf], who lived next door to us. . . . As soon as I moved to Chilmark, I started learning the language. I had to, certainly, because everybody did speak it in town" (p.56).

172. "All communication was in sign language, for it seems that none of the deaf Vineyarders read lips" (Groce, p. 57).

173. Groce, pp. 59, 60.

174. See Groce's chapter 5, "The Island Adaptation to Deafness."

175. Elaine Scarry, *On Beauty and Being Just* (Princeton: Princeton University Press, 1999), p. 31.

176. "Beauty is lifesaving . . . as in Rilke's imperative 'You must

change your life.' And Homer was right: Beauty incites deliberation, the search for precedents. But what about the immortal, about which Homer may or may not have been right? . . . [D]oes the plenitude and aspiration for truth stay stable, even if the metaphysical referent is in doubt?" (Scarry, pp. 32–33).

177. Iris Murdoch, *The Sovereignty of Good over Other Concepts* (Cambridge, UK: Cambridge University Press, 1967), pp. 86–87.

178. These terms are Scarry's from p. 113 ("all the space . . ." and "ceased to be the hero . . .") and p. 93 ("a symmetry of everyone's relation to another"). In this latter phrase Scarry is quoting John Rawls.

179. *The Nature of True Virtue* is not easy reading. See Gerald McDermott, *One Holy and Happy Society* (State College: Pennsylvania State University Press, 1992), especially chapters three and five, for the implications of Edwards's spirituality on his social ethic.

180. Todd Gitlin, "Elaine Scarry on Beauty and Being Just," *The American Prospect*, November 30, 2002.

181. There are debates about whether Jesus's family and Jesus himself were truly members of the poorest social class. Many argue that, if Jesus and his father were carpenters, they were artisans and not members of the lowest, peasant class. Certainly, Jesus was literate, and no son of a peasant-class family would have been taught to read. On the other hand, nothing like our "middle class" really existed in Galilee of Jesus time. "Not even artisans, such as carpenters or stonemasons, formed anything comparable to our middle class." (Ben Witheringon, *The Jesus Quest: The Third Search for the Jew of Nazareth* [Downers Grove, Ill.: InterVarsity Press, 1999], p. 29.) Also, Jesus would have lived his life under the opprobrium of illegitimacy. People

in small towns could not have missed the fact that Mary was pregnant before she was married, and Mark 6:2–3, in which Jesus is called "the son of Mary" rather than Joseph, is at least an insult and maybe a reference to his being born out of wedlock. So, while we cannot make the case that his family lived in dire poverty, we can't make the case that Jesus and his family were well-off and respectable. While Jesus could speak and relate to the rich and literate, he identified throughout his life and, particularly in his death, with the poor and the marginalized.

182. James M. Boice, "Illegalities of Christ's Trial," *The Gospel of John: An Expositional Commentary, Volume 5* (Grand Rapids: Zondervan, 1979), pp. 63ff.

183. Quoted in David Van Biema, "Why Did Jesus Have to Die?" in *Time*, April 12, 2004, p. 61. JoAnne Terrell was an African-American writer who rediscovered the power of the Christian story when she realized that, just like her own mother, Jesus was killed as a victim of injustice. She wrote that she always knew he suffered *for* us, but suddenly she realized he also suffered *with* us, he identified with the oppressed. Terrell's story is recounted on the same page of the *Time* story and I also cite it in my *The Reason for God* (New York: Dutton, 2008), p. 195.

184. This story was related in a sermon that I heard preached by another minister. I have not been able to verify if it was a real historical incident or a composed illustration.

ACKNOWLEDGMENTS

I dedicated this book to the deacons and deaconesses of Redeemer Presbyterian Church over the years, as well as the leaders of Hope for New York, a ministry that grew out of Redeemer and still works closely with our church (and others) to serve the poor of the city. I am also so grateful for the lifetime work and ministries of my friends and colleagues Jeff White and Mark Gornik of the New Song Churches in Harlem and Baltimore. With regard to doing justice, we have been interdependent learners for years. I sometimes taught them, and they have in turn taught me, and together we have discovered the principles and practices presented in this book.

The first church that taught me about care for the needy, however, was my congregation in Hopewell, Virginia. There, Christians knew instinctively that if love is genuine, it is expressed not simply in words but in deeds.

Acknowledgments

As usual, this book would not have been written without the editorial guidance and personal support of my agent, David McCormick, and my editor at Penguin, Brian Tart. Many thanks again to Lynn Land and Janice Worth, who year in and year out make my summer writing time possible. Janice merits special kudos for this present volume, however, because it was her idea that I turn a talk on justice and generosity into a book. Finally I thank my wife, Kathy. This volume is just one more joint effort to make good on our wedding pledge, that, through our life together, "the afflicted may hear, and be glad" (Psalm 34:2).

ABOUT THE AUTHOR

TIMOTHY KELLER was born and raised in Pennsylvania, and educated at Bucknell University, Gordon-Conwell Theological Seminary, and Westminster Theological Seminary. He was first a pastor in Hopewell, Virginia. In 1989 he started Redeemer Presbyterian Church in Manhattan, with his wife, Kathy, and their three sons. Today, Redeemer has more than five thousand regular Sunday attendees. Also the author of *Counterfeit Gods*, *The Prodigal God*, and the *New York Times* bestseller *The Reason for God*, he lives in New York with his family.